Organizational Coaching

Building Relationships and Programs that Drive Results

Virginia Bianco-Mathis, Cynthia Roman,
and Lisa Nabors

ASTD
PRESS

Alexandria, Virginia

ASTD Press is an internationally renowned source of insightful and practical information on workplace learning and performance topics, including training basics, evaluation and return-on-investment, instructional systems development, e-learning, leadership, and career development.

Ordering information: Books published by ASTD Press can be purchased by visiting our website at store.astd.org or by calling 800.628.2783 or 703.683.8100.

Library of Congress Control Number: 2007939269

ISBN-10: 1-56286-513-7
ISBN-13: 978-1-56286-513-9

ASTD Press Editorial Staff
Director: Cat Russo
Manager, Acquisitions and Author Development: Mark Morrow
Editorial Manager: Jacqueline Edlund-Braun
Senior Associate Editor: Tora Estep
Editorial Assistant: Maureen Soyars
Retail Trade Manager: Yelba Quinn

Copyeditor and Indexer: April Davis
Proofreader: Kris Patenaude
Interior Design and Production: Kathleen Schaner
Cover Design: Steve Fife
Cover Illustration: Yuri Arcurs

Printed by Victor Graphics, Inc., Baltimore, Maryland, www.victorgraphics.com

Contents

Preface

There are many books out there on the topic of coaching. A recent Google search for books on business coaching yielded over 500,000 results. So, why did we decide to write yet another book about coaching, and what makes this book different?

As behavioral practitioners, we have used coaching as an organization development tool to improve individual, team, and organizational performance. Through many years of application in private sector, government, and not-for-profit organizations, we have carefully measured our successes and mistakes. We have incorporated our learning into a model that represents best practices on many fronts.

First, we present coaching theory in combination with organizational and adult learning theory. We have provided a theoretical framework so you can consider the observations and suggestions presented herein within a larger context of human behavior and change. Second, we provide specific questions, job aids, templates, and resources to help readers design, research, present, implement, and assess a coaching program that will add value to their organizations—everything from managing organizational politics to developing coaching guidelines. Third, we outline a fluid coaching process for establishing coaching relationships, gathering supporting data, developing goals, dealing with resistance, and moving toward tangible results.

So, what didn't we do? We did not write a handbook for coaches. We do not provide an exhaustive search of the literature nor endorse one particular coaching school or style. We do not discuss individual or life coaching as it occurs outside of organizations. And we do not discuss in detail the effect of multicultural elements in the workplace. We encourage you to seek out other texts that address these topics more specifically.

We have combined the best of what we know about organizations and coaching. The reward we have seen for organizations where coaching is practiced successfully is substantial—defined purpose, dynamic relationships, and tangible results. We invite you to read this book, apply the content, and experience it for yourself.

Virginia Bianco-Mathis
Cynthia Roman
Lisa Nabors

August 2008

Introduction

Pat was an experienced, well-trained, workplace learning professional. After 20 years of successful corporate experience, she was told to add coaching to her "toolkit." The first thing she did was buy some of the latest books on coaching. All of the books told her that active listening was important to coaching. Okay, she knew how to listen. A few of the books said that good coaches ask good questions, leaving Pat to wonder: *What are good questions? When should she ask these questions?* Another book advised her to maintain confidentiality while coaching. Well, obviously, this author didn't know some of the managers in Pat's company!

As consultants and coaches each with over 20 years of corporate experience, we wanted experienced workplace learning professionals like Pat to have a model for coaching that would take into account the needs of businesses. This book provides an organizational coaching approach that is results-driven, future-focused, data-based, and action-oriented. We describe the concrete, behavior-based steps on the what and the how of coaching. In addition, we distinguish organizational coaching from the more widely known life coaching or other coaching contexts. Unlike life coaching, organizational coaching requires a systems approach in which workplace learning professionals can effectively coach individuals and teams, and even create organizational coaching cultures. This book is full of tips, advice, checklists, and assessments for coaches to use for themselves and with clients. Our integrated model enables the workplace learning and performance (WLP) professional to create desirable coaching outcomes with coaching clients, despite the constantly changing objectives in organizations.

Target Audience

People who define themselves as WLP professionals and want to add coaching to their strategic toolkits will find this book valuable. WLP professionals in organizations often provide the following:

- executive/leadership coaching
- career development
- leadership development
- professional or skill development
- performance improvement
- succession planning
- work/life balance
- stress management
- team development
- retirement planning
- executive team coaching.

We present a model for organizational coaching in this book that will provide a roadmap for any coaching role the WLP professional adopts. The elements in the model are applicable to any level of coaching relationship—individual, team, or even the entire organization.

Overview of the Book

This book will help you determine your approach to organizational coaching. Each chapter describes a specific element of the organizational coaching model, as well as the skills and strategies for applying it to a specific coaching relationship.

Chapter 1

"Coaching vs. Other Organizational Change Practices" compares coaching to four other distinct, but often confused, change practices: therapy, training, mentoring, and consulting. We define coaching and discuss a research-based, theoretical foundation for coaching that distinguishes it from pop psychology.

The questions answered in this chapter are as follows:

- What is coaching?
- How is coaching different from therapy, training, mentoring, or consulting?
- Isn't coaching just pop psychology?
- How can I use a sound, theoretical basis for my coaching?
- What is evidence-based coaching?

Chapter 2

"Defining the Role" presents and explains a holistic model of organizational coaching that provides not only a structure that the coach appreciates but also the flexibility that the coach requires. Our organizational coaching model consists of eight process and content steps that can be used when coaching involves individuals, teams, or the entire organization. The first step—defining the role—is covered in detail within this chapter.

The questions answered in this chapter are as follows:

- ▶ What are the steps in a coaching relationship?
- ▶ How does a coach use this coaching model?
- ▶ How do the steps in coaching relate to each other?
- ▶ How is a holistic model of coaching useful?
- ▶ How would these coaching steps look in an actual coaching situation?
- ▶ What are the various roles of the WLP coach?
- ▶ What are three types of organizational coaching?
- ▶ How do I match coaching services with the kind of clients I want to coach?

Chapter 3

"Building the Foundation" focuses on what to do to build a successful coaching relationship. Ethical guidelines, adapted from those of the International Coach Federation, are presented along with the elements for effective coaching agreements. We provide sample coaching agreements, tips, and checklists for building a strong coaching partnership, whether the coaching is with an individual, a team, or the organization.

The questions answered in this chapter are as follows:

- ▶ How do I know if I'm a good fit for my client?
- ▶ What questions should I be prepared to answer in an interview for a coaching assignment?
- ▶ How do I know if my client is ready for coaching?
- ▶ What are the ethical guidelines for coaching?
- ▶ What should I include in a coaching agreement with my client?

Chapter 4

"Co-Creating the Partnership" provides detailed descriptions, sample scripts, and how-to advice on the dialogue skills needed for successful coaching. You will learn how coaching dialogue is different from everyday workplace conversations and how to use the skills of dialogue to achieve desired results. Case studies will enable you to apply these skills to different coaching scenarios.

The questions answered in this chapter are as follows:

- ▸ Which powerful questions can I use to get behind the reasoning of others?
- ▸ What are the three levels of listening?
- ▸ What are the top 10 dialogue techniques I can master?
- ▸ How can I balance advocacy and inquiry?

Chapter 5

"Collecting and Analyzing Coaching Data" provides a useful overview of sources and methods for coaching data collection. Beginning with a discussion of the reasons why you might collect data, this chapter reviews the strengths and weaknesses of various tools (for example, self-assessments, 360-degree surveys, qualitative interviews) and then goes on to discuss how the tools fit with the client's organization. You will read about the process of analyzing and sorting data, extracting themes, and forming hypotheses. The topics of credibility, intent, and access are discussed, and the link among beliefs, behaviors, and results is explored.

The questions answered in this chapter are as follows:

- ▸ Why collect data?
- ▸ What data sources are available to me?
- ▸ How do I choose a data-gathering tool?
- ▸ Why should I analyze the data?
- ▸ How does sorting data affect my coaching client's learning and action?

Chapter 6

"Feeding Back Coaching Data" explores a crucial skill for the WLP coach. In this chapter, you will learn how to analyze and feed back the data in a way that will motivate the client to create and follow through on an action plan for development. Through examples and case studies, you will see how various types of data can be summarized and presented in a way that will motivate change.

The questions answered in this chapter are as follows:

- ▸ What is the relationship between context and effective feedback?
- ▸ How do I encourage reflection?
- ▸ How do I help my coaching clients see their behaviors in new ways?
- ▸ What is an informed choice, and how do I contribute to it?
- ▸ What are examples of effective feedback techniques?

Chapter 7

"Designing Goals and Tracking Progress" covers the process by which the WLP coach and client are ready to set measurable objectives and create tools to track progress toward meeting those objectives. In this chapter, we present options and strategies so your client can track progress. We provide case studies and templates for how you and your client can create a coaching action plan that is most likely to achieve your client's and your organization's goals.

The questions answered in this chapter are as follows:

- ▶ How do coaching action plans contribute to change?
- ▶ How do I help my coaching client identify goals?
- ▶ What are the elements in an effective coaching action plan?
- ▶ What can I do to support my coaching client in prioritizing actions?
- ▶ What techniques can I use to assess progress?
- ▶ In what ways can clients engage their working environments in the coaching process?

Chapter 8

"Conducting Coaching Meetings" describes how to keep the momentum going throughout the coaching partnership. Whether the coaching lasts three months or 12 months, the coach needs to know how to handle each coaching meeting, including what to do if the client does not make progress toward objectives. In this chapter we provide our COACH model, a protocol for using dialogue skills throughout a coaching meeting and the entire coaching relationship.

The questions answered in this chapter are as follows:

- ▶ How do I conduct each coaching meeting with my clients? What model do I use?
- ▶ How do I support my clients' progress toward their coaching objectives?
- ▶ How do I help my clients identify strategies to overcome barriers?
- ▶ How do I help my clients find meaning in successes and setbacks?

Chapter 9

"Managing the Coaching Program" enables you to effectively plan for and manage a successful organizational coaching program. Using a systems approach, we provide checklists and other tools for planning, marketing, developing, measuring, and publicizing results of an organizational coaching program. You will also learn how to tie the plan to organizational business needs and successfully navigate a list of common challenges. This chapter includes how to measure the return-on-investment of coaching in a way that managers can use and understand.

The questions answered in this chapter are as follows:

- ▶ What should coaching guidelines include?
- ▶ Which stakeholders should be involved in planning a coaching program?

▶ What techniques are useful in selling and negotiating a coaching program?
▶ How can program challenges be managed?
▶ What measures need to be incorporated in a coaching program?
▶ How can I build an entire coaching infrastructure?

How to Read This Book

Before you dive into this book, we suggest that you first get clarity about your organizational coaching role. Will you be coaching individuals, teams, or both? What kind of coaching will you be doing? What kind of infrastructure will support your coaching role? Answers to these questions will help you get the most out of each chapter.

You may want to read this book from start to finish, especially if you are new to your organizational coaching role. In general, the chapters follow our organizational coaching model in a linear fashion. However, in as much as coaching is iterative, so are the elements in the model. If you know which elements of the model prove most challenging to you, you may want to focus more on those particular chapters. Take notes. Think about how the ideas apply to your coaching relationships. Take the time to practice the concepts and tools within each chapter by completing the "Moving Ideas to Action" section provided at the end of each chapter.

Remember that coaching is a partnership. Ask your clients if what you are doing is helping them achieve their goals. Use your clients' feedback to help you focus on which elements of the coaching model need more attention. And finally, remember that every coaching relationship is different. Our hope is that you will come back to this book often as your coaching needs change. Have fun as you discover your path into organizational coaching!

Coaching vs. Other Organizational Change Practices

▶ the definition of coaching

▶ how coaching compares with other change practices

▶ how to use evidenced-based coaching to ground your practices in sound, theoretical knowledge

▶ cognitive approaches to coaching that create a strong coaching base and produce results

What Is Coaching?

At its heart, coaching is about change. And as most organizational learning professionals know, goals for learning and change go hand in hand. So how can coaching advance the goals for workplace learning? Recent research in the neurosciences (Rock 2006; Schwartz and Begley 2002) has shown that it doesn't take as long to neurologically create new thinking patterns and new habits as we previously thought. Positive feedback and continuous reinforcement make a tremendous difference in helping people hardwire these desirable changes in the brain and sustain them over the long term (Schwartz and Beyette 1996).

Numerous change strategies are available to the workplace learning and performance (WLP) professional at the individual, team, and organizational levels. It is important to understand how coaching

> *Coaching is partnering with clients in a thought-provoking and creative process that inspires them to maximize their personal and professional potential*
>
> —International Coach Federation (www.coachfederation.org, June 2007)

compares to these existing strategies. Some of the different strategies overlap, yet there are important distinctions. These distinctions will help you ascertain whether your coaching client can truly benefit from coaching or perhaps needs another form of development. The definitions and examples in table 1-1 compare coaching to the following change strategies: therapy, training, mentoring, and consulting.

As you can see from table 1-1, coaching differs from other related behavioral strategies and yet overlaps in some ways. You may find that coaching easily pairs with some other strategies. For example, coaching is an excellent follow-up to some training programs. And many leadership development programs include training, mentoring, and coaching. Keep in mind that coaching has more guidelines than hard and fast rules. Consider how you can make coaching work in your organization.

> *Coaching helps people think better. The person being coached is the expert in their work—the coach uses a questioning approach to help the person find their own answers.*
>
> —David Rock
> (www.workplacecoaching.com, June 2007)

Once you have distinguished the uniqueness of coaching in relationship to other organizational change strategies, you should begin to define exactly what coaching means to you. Given the explosive popularity of coaching, you can find numerous resources, definitions, and models. You will find it useful to start your own library of coaching resources, tools, and references. Different authors have different perspectives and theories. Develop your own way of thinking about coaching by integrating several approaches and adding your own ideas.

If we look for themes in the definitions of organizational coaching throughout the chapter, you might note the emphasis on partnership or relationship between the coach and the client. It is also evident that organizational coaching focuses on both organizational goals and personal needs. You may note other points that hold interest for you in your organizational coaching role.

> *In co-active coaching, this relationship is an alliance between two equals for the purpose of meeting the client's needs.*
>
> —Whitworth, Kimsey-House, Kimsey-House, and Sandahl
> (Co-Active Coaching, 2007, 3)

Theory and Practice of Coaching

A growing number of WLP professional coaches argue for what is termed *evidence-based coaching*. "The term *evidence-based coaching* was coined by Grant (2003) to distinguish between professional coaching that is explicitly grounded in a broader

Table 1-1. Coaching versus Other Behavioral Strategies.

Coaching	Therapy
• Focuses on goals, results, and development • Is future-focused and action-oriented • Builds on a person's strengths • Is based on assignments that forward the action toward objectives • Involves a balance of inquiry to encourage thinking and advocacy (making evidence-based statements) to test for understanding and agreement	• Focuses on problems and pathologies and understanding the past • Is based on personal discussion and insights • Emphasizes feelings more than reasoning
Example: LeeAnn participates in her company's leadership development program. One of the program's tools was an emotional intelligence assessment that gave her feedback on her strengths and challenges as they related to her leadership competencies. She set goals with a leadership coach on how she could leverage her strengths and improve in her challenge areas. She now knows what she needs to do to achieve her career goals in the next five years.	**Example:** Pat could be a candidate for a leadership position in her company. However, she has developed a reputation for being a loose cannon. She easily becomes angry and volatile and has embarrassed herself and others on several occasions. Lately, she has developed a drinking problem. She can't seem to get control of her problem on her own and doesn't know why she gets so angry so easily.

Coaching	Training
• Is individualized, tailored, and customized to the individual • Is based on gathered data on one particular individual or team • Requires individual progress and measurement • Involves an ongoing timeframe, using powerful questions for learning	• Addresses generic skills and expectations for the client organization • Involves a shorter timeframe than coaching • Measures progress toward generic skill sets offered in the training
Example: A team asks a coach to help it transition to working with a new software system. The team has to develop new ways of working together and across team boundaries. The coach gathers data from team members, as well as stakeholders, to help the team set objectives and create an action plan.	**Example:** A team is adapting to a new software system. They attend a two-day training class on the new system, which includes both technical and application protocols.

Coaching	Mentoring
• Balances individual and organizational goals • Requires powerful questions • Can occur between peers • Focuses on learning	• Emphasizes organizational goals • Occurs between a senior and a junior employee • Focuses on career development • Involves the giving of advice
Example: Walter has a career coach who helps him identify his strengths, weaknesses, interests, and needs. They explore various areas for a career transition.	**Example:** Patricia has a mentor in her field of wildlife management, and he is helping her identify what certifications and training she needs to advance in her organization.

(continued on next page)

Table 1-1. Coaching versus Other Behavioral Strategies (continued).

Coaching	Consulting
• Uses data to set goals • Deepens learning to forward action • Emphasizes personal change • Moves toward making the client accountable for results	• Focuses on problem solving • Uses data to diagnose problems • Emphasizes group or organizational change • Accepts the consultant as the expert
Example: Li's coach conducts an image study to determine how she is perceived by members of her team. The data will either confirm or disconfirm Li's belief that she provides excellent development and participative opportunities to her team members.	**Example:** Yusuf hires an information technology consultant to determine why the various systems are not providing the kind of data the chief executive officer needs to make certain financial decisions.

Adapted with permission from Bianco-Mathis, Nabors, and Roman (2002, 5).

> *Executive coaching is . . . a collaborative, individualized relationship between an executive and a coach, the aims of which are to bring about sustained behavioral change and to transform the quality of the executive's working and personal life.*
>
> —Zeus and Skiffington (*The Complete Guide to Coaching at Work*, 2000, 9)

empirical and theoretical knowledge base and coaching that is evolved from the 'pop psychology' personal development genre" (Stober and Grant 2006).

Most coaches agree that part of their role is to serve as caring, compassionate partners in the coaching relationship. A cognitive approach requires that they also be thought partners. Coaches who use cognitive approaches assist their clients to identify errors in their thinking and aid them in adopting more accurate, useful reasoning and thinking patterns. Coaches who adopt cognitive approaches (influenced primarily by Burns [1980], Ellis [1979], and Argyris [1990]) believe that eliminating thinking errors leads to better relationships with others, improved decision making, and higher levels of performance (Stober and Grant 2006).

> *Executive coaching is an experiential and individualized leader development process that builds a leader's capability to achieve short- and long-term organizational goals. It is conducted through one-on-one interactions, driven by data from multiple perspectives, and based on mutual trust and respect. The organization, an executive, and the executive coach work in partnership to achieve maximum impact.*
>
> —Executive Coaching Forum (*The Executive Coaching Handbook,* www.executivecoachingforum.com, 2007)

Perhaps the most powerful cognitive tool in coaching is the mental model. Mental models are our beliefs about how the world works and how people operate. Mental models can be useful, or they can get in the way of our progress toward our goals because they may limit us to habitual ways of thinking. Some examples of mental models are, "People can't be trusted," "If I graduate, I'll get a good job," "Only technical people get ahead here," and "Being controlling is the only way to get things done." Coaches can have a powerful effect on their clients by questioning mental models in the coaching dialogue. A process for addressing mental models during a coaching conversation would include recognizing the mental models at play, understanding how unexamined mental models are affecting the client's decision making and behavior, learning how to slow down and reflect on mental models, and engaging in conversations that test assumptions and inferences (Auerback 2006, 114).

> *Coaching is . . . challenging and supporting people in achieving higher levels of performance while allowing them to bring out the best in themselves and those around them.*
>
> —Hargrove (*Masterful Coaching* 1995, 15)

Another useful tool that can be used in helping clients become aware of their thought processes and the effects on their behaviors is the ladder of inference, as shown in table 1-2. The ladder of inference is a tool you can use to help your clients see how they often make subjective interpretations or inferences from an observation that leads to an inaccurate conclusion or behavior. When you use the ladder of inference in your coaching, you help your clients discover errors in their reasoning and ways to prevent and re-evaluate resulting behaviors and actions—in essence, ways to stop the unconscious mind from falling into the same conclusions again and again.

> *Leadership coaching is . . . based on the commitment to align beliefs with actions. Coaching leaders communicate powerfully, help others to create desired outcomes, and hold relationships based on honesty, acceptance, and accountability.*
>
> —Bianco-Mathis, Nabors, and Roman (*Leading From the Inside Out: A Coaching Model*, 2002, 4)

You can see how this works by studying the example in table 1-2. Given Susan's one experience with a working mother, Susan assumes all working mothers are the same. This affects her behavior to the point that she does not reward nor hire working mothers. Whenever she

> *Workplace coaching . . . takes place in workplace settings with non-executive employees, and includes on-the-job coaching by line managers and supervisors with the aim of improving productivity and developing an individual worker's skills and understanding of job requirements.*
>
> —Cavanaugh and Grant ("Executive Coaching in Organizations: The Personal Is the Professional," *The International Journal of Coaching in Organizations*, 2:7–8)

Table 1-2. Ladder of Inference.

Action Take action based on beliefs.	Susan gives Tom and Lakeisha better job assignments; her next hire is a middle-aged person with grown kids; she does not offer Laura any promotions.
Belief Adopt beliefs about the world.	Susan believes that working moms are not a good fit for her team and decides to keep this in mind when hiring people.
Conclusions Draw conclusions.	Susan concludes that she is better off developing Tom and Lakeisha because she can rely on them.
Assumptions Make assumptions based on the added meanings.	Susan assumes she can't rely on Laura.
Meaning Add meanings (cultural and personal).	Laura doesn't make her job a priority. She has trouble managing her life every morning with getting her kids off to school. She isn't organized.
Selected Data Select data from what is observed.	Susan notices that Laura again saunters in 15 minutes late. This is the third time she has come in late with no explanation.
Observable Data Observe data and experiences.	Susan holds weekly scheduled staff meetings.

"Ladder of inference" adapted from Peter Senge et al., *The Fifth Discipline Fieldbook* (New York: Doubleday, 1994), p. 243; see also McArthur, Putnam, and Smith (1999).

encounters a working mother, Susan immediately climbs her ladder of inference and reinforces her original belief—despite any information to the contrary.

All of us climb up our ladders of inference hundreds of times every day, usually unaware that we are going through the process. During coaching conversations, we can help our clients slow down their thinking long enough to reflect on their reasoning and the effect their choices have on themselves and others.

These two cognitive tools—mental model and ladder of inference—represent the kind of theoretical underpinnings that support the organizational coaching model outlined in chapter 2. The use of these and other cognitive models presented in this book will help you create a strong coaching base, move beyond superficial coaching practices, and produce evidence-based results.

Moving Ideas to Action

Refer to table 1-2. Think of a workplace conversation or situation that did not go as you would have liked. Fill in table 1-3 with your own example of the ladder of inference, applying your reasoning from the example you have chosen. Then consider the questions below.

Table 1-3. My Ladder of Inference.

My Ladder of Inference	My Reasoning at Each Rung of the Ladder
Actions	
Beliefs	
Conclusions	
Assumptions	
Meanings	
Selected Data	
Observable Data and Experiences	

1. Did you achieve what you wanted out of this conversation or situation? Why or why not?
2. What might an alternative be to the reasoning you had at each rung? How would the outcome have differed if you had used that alternative reasoning?

2

Defining the Role

.... **In this chapter, you'll learn** ....

▷ the organizational coaching model, a holistic approach that provides both the structure and flexibility that coaching requires

▷ a detailed explanation of the eight steps that make up the organizational coaching model

▷ how the eight steps of the model look in an actual coaching situation

The Organizational Coaching Model

What is unique about this model is its holistic nature. The depiction of the yin and the yang of the coaching steps reflects the dualistic yet complementary nature of how coaching works. This model has both process and content steps that should be followed in all organizational coaching contexts, whether coaching an individual, a team, or an organization. The steps, flowing back and forth from process to content, create a harmony that is unique to each coaching partnership. Also, as shown in figure 2-1, the entire coaching process is designed to support a program that is carefully planned and managed. Although we portray each step building on the preceding one, the continuous and organic nature of coaching is more fluid than lock-step in practice. As you proceed in your coaching relationship, you will probably engage with the coaching model elements in an iterative fashion. For example, you may collect and feed back data at several points in the coaching relationship. Or, you may have reason to revisit your coaching agreements from time to time. It is also not uncommon to measure and track results regularly and in different ways throughout the coaching process, not just at the end of the relationship.

Figure 2-1. Organizational Coaching Model.

CONTENT	PROCESS
Defining the Role	Building the Foundation
Collecting and Analyzing Coaching Data	Co-Creating the Partnership
Designing Goals and Tracking Progress	Feeding Back Coaching Data
Managing the Coaching Program	Conducting Coaching Meetings

Adapted from *The Organizational Coaching Model*, Bianco-Mathis, Nabors, and Roman (2007).

A narrative description of each component of the model follows. This includes an explanation of the component and the rationale for its placement in the content or process side of the model.

Defining the Role

Explanation: Coaches assess their coaching roles within the organization, who will be coached, possible coaching scenarios, and the coaching guidelines that need to be followed.

This content step is essential as a first activity to center yourself and focus the coaching you will be conducting (or want to conduct) within an organization. Are you full time or part time? Are you a manager who also functions as a coach, or are you an outside practitioner hired by the organization for coaching purposes? Will you be coaching executives or dealing only with problem employees? It is important to understand, communicate, and reach agreement on the expectations of your coaching role. Various organizations have developed different coaching guidelines that you will need to follow and uphold. It is also essential that you test the alignment of the organization's coaching structure with your own sense of ethics, approach, skills, tools, and purpose.

Building the Foundation

Explanation: The coach and client develop agreements that will guide the coaching relationship.

At the onset of the coaching relationship, you should be focused on building the foundation for an effective partnership with your client. By creating an agreement regarding mutual roles and responsibilities during the coaching partnership, you build trust and avoid confusion and misunderstandings that can occur later on. This agreement covers topics such as confidentiality, scheduling, absences, and accountability and answers any other questions either of you have.

Building the foundation for a successful coaching relationship is an ideal example of an ongoing process. Coaches are constantly engaged in building trust, clarifying roles, encouraging accountability, and other aspects of the coaching partnership. This process ebbs and flows with the growth in the relationship and progress toward results.

Co-Creating the Partnership

Explanation: The coach establishes trust and uses language that leads to higher levels of understanding, insight, and action.

You will be communicating with your client in a very different way from normal workplace communication. In coaching conversations, the coach uses a combination of listening, advocacy (guiding), inquiry (meaningful questioning), and other powerful dialogue techniques that lead to higher levels of understanding, insight, and awareness.

Co-creating the partnership is a process step in the coaching model because communication is a process that cannot be precisely defined or predicted. The coaching dialogue is complex and dynamic. Depending on the coach's skillfulness, the client's readiness, and other variables, insights and results will vary.

Collecting and Analyzing Coaching Data

Explanation: The coach collects data regarding the client's current effectiveness and analyzes the data for strengths and areas for improvement.

This step in the organizational coaching model is what distinguishes organizational coaching from life coaching and other coaching contexts. Data will inform your thinking in several areas and will allow you to best support your client. You will have access to behavioral information, information about your client's intentions, others' perceptions, and overall results. When you collect data and identify themes and patterns, you can shine a light on what your clients are creating for themselves and others within their organizations. Collecting data allows you to identify with greater certainty your clients' areas of strength and what areas, if any, are causing them to be less effective than they would like. You may not be expected to conduct a large, sophisticated, organization-wide climate survey. However, you should know how to conduct interviews and smaller surveys for coaching data collection. You should also be able to do content analysis for themes to feed back data to your coaching client.

In organizations, each person's actions have a far-reaching effect. When it comes to assessing how your clients are being perceived in the organization and how people are experiencing them, data allow you and your clients to take the guesswork out of the coaching process. Collecting and analyzing coaching data are presented as a content step because of its clear focus on data.

Feeding Back Coaching Data

Explanation: The coach communicates a summary of the collected data to the client in a way that motivates positive action.

This step in the organizational coaching model has the most direct effect on your clients' abilities to make informed choices regarding their actions. Your objective is to help your clients understand the data you collected, consider the risks and rewards of action (or inaction), and move forward by setting objectives for development. Be prepared to deal with resistance in its many forms—from outright rejection to passivity to intellectualizing. Your job as coach is to help your client deal with resistance and get past it.

This step is represented as a process step because of the interaction between you and your client, including the choice points that are experienced during the coaching dialogue. While the coaching clients are ultimately responsible for the choices they make, as the coach, you are responsible for feeding back data in such a way that the clients hear the information, explore several perspectives, and are willing to consider and select from several courses of action.

Designing Goals and Tracking Progress

Explanation: The coach and client create an action plan built on objectives. They meet regularly to track progress and dialogue about learning and results.

Once your clients have considered their feedback, they will decide where they want to focus their energy. In this step of the organizational coaching model, you will help your clients identify specific goals and create action plans that will move them forward. The action plan document, in whatever format the client chooses, will enable you both to track progress toward identified goals and inform your coaching conversations. These conversations should focus on progress and learning whether the client is describing a success or a setback. Supports and strategies can be identified in either circumstance and are useful in helping the client plan for future efforts.

Tracking progress starts at the beginning of the coaching process when you and your clients identify what to accomplish through coaching and what will be different when they do so. Frequently, clients will define short- and long-term goals, and you may use a combination of quantitative and qualitative measures to assess progress throughout the coaching relationship. You might use the same 360-degree survey to measure both pre- and post-coaching behaviors. Or, you might have your client complete a self-evaluation to rate effectiveness in defined areas before, during, and after coaching. This step is presented as a content step because it is focused on identified goals, agreed-upon actions, and analysis of results.

Conducting Coaching Meetings

Explanation: Although the client sets the agenda for each coaching meeting, the coach provides structure and process.

Your initial agreement with your client will determine how often you will meet and how long your partnership will last. You should give your client the opportunity to set the agenda at each meeting and be sure to track progress toward the agreed-upon objectives. You will provide a structure and process for the meeting, ending with commitments for action. You should use a model to structure each meeting, such as the COACH model discussed in chapter 8. Since change is rarely smooth, you need to be prepared to deal with clients who get stuck along the way to achieving their coaching objectives.

Conducting coaching meetings, like co-creating the partnership, is considered a process step. The quality of the interaction between coach and client, the ebb and flow of the dialogue, the learning that occurs each time the coach and client are together, and the learning that occurs when the client is alone are rooted in process.

Managing the Coaching Program

Explanation: This step includes all of the upfront design and coordination with stakeholders, planning, implementation, and ongoing administration and maintenance.

Although creating a master plan is the first activity that must be done before even implementing a coaching program, we cover it last as a way to provide structure to the entire model. Managing the coaching program is a content step that holds all the pieces imbedded within the entire model—and it is ongoing because you must manage and track a coaching program from beginning to end on a regular basis. The master plan for a coaching program includes a clearly defined vision, guidelines, steps, protocols, contingencies, alignment, and agreements. All stakeholders must be involved to establish buy-in, support, open communication, and alignment with other related programs within the organization.

Managing the coaching program is represented as a content step because certain basic elements must be in place for an organizational coaching program to be successful. In chapter 9, we discuss these elements and how to take a systems approach in creating the master plan.

The following case is an example of a coaching partnership that depicts all of the steps in our holistic coaching model. As you read through this case, see if you can identify the elements of the organizational coaching model.

Mark's Case

Two years ago, under the direction of the vice president of human resources at Future Life Inc. (FLI), an insurance company, the company formed a Coaching Task Force (CTF) as a way to plan, implement, and manage a coaching program and approach throughout all divisions at all locations.

The CTF spent six meetings designing an overall coaching program for the organization. It established a guidelines booklet that addressed essential topics such as program purpose; benefits for individuals, teams, and the entire organization; roles, expectations, and agreements; confidentiality; external and internal coaches; and protocol for tracking and measuring results. It conducted group introductory sessions, distributed the guidelines, sent out a newsletter, and posted pertinent information on the company intranet. Working through the CTF and Executive Committee, human resources proposed and received support to build coaching into performance development, career development, training, quality improvement, and other systems to create a coordinated approach toward personal and organizational success.

Each department within the company took the CTF guidelines and created its own task force to drive coaching all the way down the organization. In particular, the call centers created their own Call Center Coaching (CCC) Task Force to develop a coaching approach for customer care advisors and the call representatives. Already established within the call centers was a quality assessment and feedback mechanism for giving performance feedback to the call representatives. Managers and supervisors within the call centers saw the new coaching approach as a way to raise the effectiveness of this practice. Consequently, the CCC Task Force created a coaching vision and guidelines. It trained the customer care advisors in coaching techniques and then held information sessions with the call representatives to explain the process and gain buy-in and acceptance of the entire effort.

Two months ago, Mark (a customer care advisor) began coaching a new direct sales and service representative, Linda. Mark spent time building a foundation with Linda. They discussed schedules, meeting times, agreements for communicating, and expectations. Linda and Mark struck an immediate rapport. Although Linda was first concerned with confidentiality and how this would all be coordinated with her supervisor, Mark assured her that nothing personal would be shared with anyone else within the organization unless they decided together that certain information would be shared.

Mark collated data on Linda's performance through direct observation, the monthly technical assessments, and a supervisory report. He fed the data to Linda by organizing all the information into themes and specific areas that Linda could understand and move toward action.

During two pivotal coaching meetings, Mark was able to co-create a strong partnership by asking Linda a series of probing questions to help her explore her strengths and development areas. Mark used a comfortable and supportive dialogue approach. This allowed Linda to feel safe and explore alternative actions.

Overall, Linda was performing well and had two major areas that required improvement. One, she didn't ask enough questions. She would answer the immediate expressed needs of the caller but often failed to explore other areas of interest and potential sales. Two, she wasn't up-to-speed on two popular products and, therefore, spent too much time researching and having to get back to the client.

Linda realized that her desire to complete each call in a timely fashion prevented her from asking more questions and surfacing other concerns. She realized that if she mastered the product information, she could cut down on her research time and would be able to concentrate more on each call. Mark helped Linda develop an action plan that outlined steps for improving her questioning techniques and learning the product material. Mark and Linda reviewed this action plan every week and tracked progress. Linda also developed a checklist of questions that she began to use for each call so she and Mark could note her progress. Mark advised Linda to keep a learning journal as she studied the product information booklets. She discussed this with Mark and her supervisor. Linda gained confidence, and Mark was able to support her, making sure her actions were being tracked and continually aligned with her goals and call center standards.

Soon Linda became proficient in product knowledge, and her questioning techniques improved greatly. At one of the call center staff meetings, Linda shared the key client question checklist she had developed. Her supervisor and other call representatives really liked the tool, and it soon became a standard job aid throughout the call centers. Mark realized that he helped not only Linda achieve her goals but also the entire department and organization reach their yearly goals.

Coaching and System Integration

A coaching program and a workplace learning and performance (WLP) coach must work with other programs in the organization. This kind of linking among programs, strategies, and activities is referred to as a "systems model." With most systems, one component affects other components. You cannot plop a coaching program into an organization and expect it to work without linking it to other learning and program efforts within the organization.

Consequently, when working as a WLP coach, you need to link programs to maximize results and navigate organizational politics. Shelley Gaynes (2004) explains how certified coaches at IBM teach coaching skills and techniques to their American Sales Transformation Team. To simulate real-world scenarios, they use web conferences and case studies. The coaching approach is emphasized in the performance appraisal system, and specific training programs are offered on listening, open-ended questions, trust-building, and dialogue techniques. Another great linking example is offered by Anna Banks at the Canadian Centre for Management Development. Public service senior executives within the program acquire their knowledge from a multiprogram approach that includes mentors, executive advisors, personal coaches, small learning groups, and individuals who have varied job experiences (2007).

We'll talk more at length about how to navigate these complex organizational systems when planning your coaching program in chapter 9. Some of the other programs that may make up your system are depicted in figure 2-2.

Another systems concept imbedded within the organizational coaching model is the value in using the model whether you are coaching an individual, a team, or an entire organization. Building a foundation, collecting data, feeding back data, designing goals, and tracking progress must be applied within all three coaching situations. Specific tools and approaches may vary, but the actual steps must take place. For example, you might use a 360-degree survey to gather data about an individual, yet choose to use a team self-assessment when coaching a group. For an organization, the choice might be a climate survey. In the case study, Mark begins by coaching an individual—Linda. Linda then uses her new skills to increase the effectiveness of her team, which leads to a new standard for call centers throughout the entire company. This demonstrates the power of coaching as an organization development tool.

The Coaching Role

Before delving into the more interactive steps of the coaching process, let's look more closely as the first content step of the model—defining the role. WLP professionals are people working within organizations (as full-time employees or consultants) who are dedicated to advancing learning as part of their jobs. A WLP coach can be a

Figure 2-2. Organizational Coaching Model.

full-time coaching professional or a manager or other work professional who has been trained to coach others within the organization. For example, a large organization may have several trained coaches on staff within the human resources department who coach individuals and teams full time. However, a smaller company may have several dedicated managers who serve as coaches when needed. A WLP coach is presented with myriad coaching roles and scenarios.

Coaching Roles

A list of coaching roles is below. See how closely any of these examples resemble your coaching role in your organization:

- a full-time trainer who acts as an internal coach when assigned
- an outside professional coach who has a contract with an organization to serve as a coach for leaders
- a manager who has studied the coaching process and decides to run his or her department using coaching principles
- a company president who believes that coaching is the key to high performance and decides to use a style of coaching leadership to enhance the company's customer-service ratings
- a full-time, internal organizational coach
- a human resource employee who acts as an internal coach when assigned.

Coaching Scenarios

A list of coaching scenarios is below. See how closely any of these examples resemble your coaching scenarios in your organization:

- a mid-level manager who wants to develop leadership competencies to further his career
- an employee who feels stuck in her job and doesn't know how to re-energize
- a mid-level manager who is identified as "high potential"
- a leader who is receiving feedback on being too authoritative in his approach
- a team that is undergoing a transition in terms of members and mission
- an employee who receives survey feedback and three follow-up coaching sessions as part of the company's formal performance appraisal process
- an employee who wants to strengthen interpersonal skills
- a newly formed cross-functional team that wants to set itself up for success.

By now you're probably getting the picture that coaching comes in many shapes and sizes. Variations of coaching tend to break out within the following four dimensions:

external vs. internal coaches, types of training and certification, types of coaching performed, and types of clients. There is great overlap, but the distinctions matter as you reflect on your preferred area of work and skills and define your particular role as a WLP coach.

Types of Coaches

There are independent, external coaches who are hired by organizations to coach leaders and staff within the organization. External coaches are most commonly used for higher-level positions or for companies that don't have the resources to support their own internal coaching programs. External coaches typically have backgrounds that include education and experience in business and organization development, as well as organizational coaching. There are also experienced and trained internal coaches who work within organizations. Internal coaches often reside in the human resources or training department of their organizations.

Although organizational size often dictates the availability of internal coaching resources, there are other factors to consider. Being external to the organization can be advantageous to the coach and the client by offering the real or perceived sense of safety. It is not unusual to hear organizational leaders say that their coaches are the only people they feel they can talk to. However, the internal coach better understands the complex organizational systems and politics affecting how people work and behave. Regardless of whether you are external or internal, organizational coaching is always a partnership among the client, the coach, and other key stakeholders in the organization. This requires astute understanding of organizational dynamics by the coach.

Training and Certification

Some practicing coaches have gone through extensive programs from which they emerge as certified coaches. Such programs are frequently recognized by the International Coach Federation (ICF, www.coachfederation.org), a membership organization that provides resources and accreditation in the field of coaching. These programs involve years of training and practice, include tests and exams, and require ongoing study over time. Other coaches may have an advanced degree in psychology, human resource development, or leadership and may have attended one of many training courses or workshops to hone their skills around the coaching process. These programs do not lead to a certified coach designation under ICF guidelines. Still other coaches have a master's degree or certificate in coaching, often offered within a university setting. Lastly, there are individuals within organizations—managers, human resource professionals, leaders—who have excellent interpersonal skills, have natural coaching talent, and are educated by the organization to take on coaching.

Types of Coaching

Coaches tend to specialize in a particular kind of coaching or approach. In organizations, a good coach will be comfortable and skilled in integrating aspects from all three areas described below.

Leadership and executive coaching is dedicated to the needs, competencies, and concerns of executives leading an organization or large endeavor. The engagement may touch on the executive's career, work/life balance, or some particular behavioral or communication opportunity. A partnership is formed among the executive, the coach, and the organization. The individual goals of an executive coaching engagement must always link back and be subordinated to strategic organizational objectives (Executive Coaching Forum, *The Executive Coaching Handbook*, 2007, 23).

Career coaching concentrates on the world of work; explores areas in which to achieve success along a particular career path; and focuses on providing support and guidance as an individual moves from one job, level, organization, or environment to another. Career coaching emphasizes a holistic alignment of work values with personal life values and interests.

Performance coaching emphasizes the coaching skills and behaviors that help create client learning and enjoyment necessary to close the gap between the present and the desired level of job performance. Coaches work with employees, bosses, and others in their workplace to help the employees identify these performance gaps and develop action plans for further professional development.

Types of Clients

Many new coaches make the mistake of focusing solely on who they want to coach ("I want to coach CEOs!") or one particular type of coaching ("I want to do executive coaching!"). It's important to realize that the type of client you may coach in your organization depends, to a certain extent, on the type of coaching performed. Table 2-1 is a chart matching potential coaching clients and possible coaching services. Keep in mind that certain types of clients may prefer internal or external coaches. You may want to think about the business opportunities and training implications that this chart presents. For example, if you are expected to coach managers, you will likely need to be proficient in all three types of coaching: leadership, career, and performance.

Two main topics are emphasized in this chapter: the organizational coaching model and your role as a coach. In other words, what you do and who you are! The organizational coaching model provides a holistic approach to both the process and the content of coaching in workplace settings. As a workplace coaching professional, you need to carefully consider your underlying experience and training, your role as external or internal, the types of coaching you prefer, and the clients you may encounter.

Table 2-1. Matching Coaching Clients and Services.

Types of Clients	Leadership/ Executive Coaching	Career Coaching	Performance Coaching
Boards of Directors	X		
Leaders	X	X	X
Executive Teams	X		
Teams, Groups, and Task Forces	X		X
Managers	X	X	X
Staff Below Leadership Level	X	X	X
Colleagues and Associates	X	X	X
Subordinates	X	X	X
An Entire Organization	X		X

Moving Ideas to Action

Let's revisit Mark's case, which depicts all the steps and concepts within the holistic organizational coaching model. In table 2-2, give examples from the case that support the designated model component. Then, in the last column, give examples from your own organization. If you cannot give an example, note the gap or missing element. In chapter 9, we will address how to build and implement a successful program, and you can use this initial analysis as a working document.

Table 2-2. Model Application Exercise.

Model Components	Examples from Mark's Case	Examples from Your Organization
1. Defining the Role What is Mark's role in the organization—How does he function as a coach? What are his skills? What kind of coaching does he conduct?		
2. Building the Foundation How does Mark build rapport with Linda?		
3. Co-Creating the Partnership What dialogue techniques does Mark use with Linda? What is his intention?		
4. Collecting and Analyzing Coaching Data What methods does Mark use to collect data in his coaching relationship with Linda?		
5. Feeding Back Coaching Data What approach does Mark take in feeding back his data to Linda? What is the outcome of that meeting?		
6. Designing Goals and Tracking Progress What goals do Linda and Mark establish? How do they track progress toward those goals?		
7. Conducting Coaching Meetings How does Linda benefit from her ongoing coaching meetings with Mark? What techniques encourage ongoing progress toward her objectives?		
8. Managing the Coaching Program What are some of the features of how FLI manages its coaching program?		
9. Systems Approach How does Mark use a systems approach in coaching Linda?		

Building the Foundation

.... **In this chapter, you'll learn** ....

▶ the process for building a successful coaching relationship

▶ how to prepare for your first meeting or interview with a prospective client

▶ how to determine if the client is ready for coaching and if you will be a good fit with the client

▶ ethical standards for coaches

Introduction: Jennifer's Case

Walter is vice president for a large, professional services corporation. Despite a career of over 25 years at the company, he has performed less than satisfactory in the last few years. Changes in mission and stakeholder expectations have been a source of deep disappointment to Walter. He has had difficulty adjusting to new performance expectations, and he believes the company is making dire strategic mistakes. He resents that the chief executive officer (CEO) no longer listens to him and that he no longer feels valued for his services.

Jennifer is a new internal coach based in the human resources department. She has had one previous client, a team leader in the finance department. Jennifer has had five years of experience in the company, her first job out of graduate school. She has an advanced degree in human resources and experience in employee relations. She has taken a couple of courses in coaching at a local university. The CEO recently asked Jennifer to coach Walter to be more on board with the new company direction.

Figure 3-1. Organizational Coaching Model.

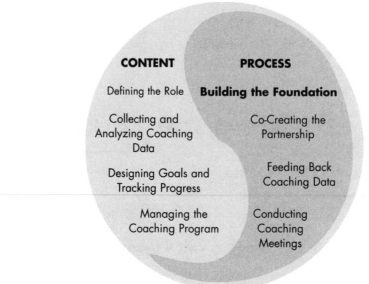

Adapted from *The Organizational Coaching Model*, Bianco-Mathis, Nabors, and Roman (2007).

During Jennifer's meeting with the CEO, he also informed her that Walter has a drinking problem and that he had a complaint filed against him for sexual harassment. The CEO said that if Walter didn't improve his performance in the next six months, he would be fired. When Jennifer asked, the CEO admitted that he has not shared this potential consequence with Walter, but that he would prefer thinking positively about Walter's potential for improvement with coaching.

During Jennifer's first meeting with Walter, she found him to be pleasant and receptive to a coaching relationship. However, Walter spent most of the hour-long meeting complaining about how the problem was the strategic direction of the company and how resentful he was that his contributions were no longer valued. Jennifer found it difficult to stop the flow of his comments long enough to set up meetings and logistics. Walter said that he would prefer meeting Jennifer after work hours at the restaurant down the street because he is so busy. Jennifer initially agreed to this request. When Jennifer suggested an interviewing process to gather feedback from others, Walter said, "Sure. You'll find that all my working relationships are excellent. The CEO just doesn't understand how good my work really is." Jennifer ended the meeting by offering to write the questions she would ask when interviewing Walter's direct reports and colleagues.

If you are speculating that Jennifer's coaching relationship with Walter is not getting off on the right foot, you are right! Building a solid foundation for the coaching relationship is critical and contributes to successful performance outcomes. It is important to determine if the client is ready, willing, and able to be coached. You and your client should spend adequate time at the beginning of the relationship making agreements about how you will work together effectively. Such agreements should include expectations, activities, roles, responsibilities, mutual accountabilities, logistics, and planning considerations. This will help prevent misunderstanding or confusion later on. And it is critical to discuss ethical considerations to help you prevent missteps that can result in awkward, ethical, or even legal consequences. Building the foundation for a successful coaching relationship does not happen in one sitting—it is a process that is often revisited and developed over time. Consequently, this activity is presented within the process side of the organizational coaching model in figure 3-1. Throughout this chapter, we will refer to Jennifer's potential coaching problems and what she might have done differently to ensure that Walter achieves his goals.

The Right Fit

The right fit between coach and client is necessary for a successful coaching relationship, whether the coaching client is an individual, a team, or the entire organization. In table 3-1, we identify some of the elements to consider for determining the right fit in a coaching relationship.

Table 3-1. Elements of Fit in a Coaching Relationship.

Coaching Client	Element
Organization	Personality/culture Work experience Organizational performance issues Organization's mission Organization development experience Others?
Team	Personality Team coaching experience Team performance issues Work experience Others?
Individual	Personality Work experience Coaching experience Education Gender Age Others?

Notice that some elements are necessary to address for a good coaching fit no matter what level you are coaching in the organization. It stands to reason that personality is important in all three levels. A sales organization that is primarily extraverted and action-oriented would probably not work well at any level with a coach who is introverted, highly reflective, and thinking-oriented. However, while age and gender may be important to consider for individual coaching, it may not be so important for coaching at the team or organizational levels. Is Jennifer a good fit to coach Walter in the case at the beginning of this chapter? Given Jennifer's relative lack of coaching experience, she may not be the best fit. She demonstrated this lack of experience by not engaging in more dialogue with the CEO and by not establishing boundaries (for example, the meeting time and location) with Walter.

Interviews Between Coaches and Clients

Ideally, a coaching client should have the opportunity to interview several prospective coaches to determine the right fit. Of course, we realize this may not be possible in some organizational coaching programs. Even if a pre-determined coaching match is made, the coach should be prepared to answer the following questions during an interview or first meeting with the coaching client:

- What is coaching?
- What experience have you had in coaching?
- What's your business background?
- How did you get into coaching?
- What skills or expertise do you have?
- What kind of coaching training have you had?
- What experience do you have with my issues?
- What managerial levels have you worked with?
- How many coaching clients have you had?
- What is your focus or philosophy of coaching?
- What do you expect of me?
- How often should we meet?
- What is your approach for each coaching session?
- Can I communicate with you between coaching sessions?
- How confidential are our conversations?
- What kinds of clients do you prefer to work with?
- What kinds of clients do you not work effectively with?
- What kind of communication will you have with my boss?
- How will I know if the coaching has been successful?

From what we know about Jennifer and Walter's first meeting, it does not appear that Walter had any questions about Jennifer or the coaching relationship. This should have been a red flag for Jennifer. She then should have taken the initiative to open dialogue about the meaning of coaching, mutual roles and responsibilities, and expectations and agreements. Walter appeared to be pursuing a different agenda, and Jennifer did not take control of the process.

Client Readiness

Building a good foundation for a successful coaching relationship requires assessing not only the elements of a good fit and successfully answering interview questions, but also client readiness for coaching. After all, coaching is a partnership, and both parties have responsibilities toward achieving the stated objectives. The client has actions to accomplish, and the coach has processes to control and monitor.

The ideal scenario from the perspective of readiness is when the client wants to engage in a coaching relationship and personally reaches out to a coach. The other extreme—and one that every coach dreads—is the client who is resistant to coaching or is forced to be in a coaching relationship. Before you jump to the conclusion that coaching will not work with this client, try asking the following questions:

- ▶ If you were open to coaching, what would be your goals?
- ▶ How willing would you be to commit to these expectations if there was a high probability you could achieve the desired goals you just stated?
- ▶ What kind of agreements could you and I make that would create the kind of coaching relationship that would be comfortable for you?

Using questions such as these can move the client toward a higher state of readiness. The evolution of coaching has seen a shift from using coaching to fix performance problems to using coaching as a developmental tool focusing on future goals. Although some organizations still require employees to participate in coaching, it is often a prescription for failure because it is reminiscent of the old performance improvement mentality.

Another indicator of readiness for coaching is the client's willingness to make coaching meetings and the work between meetings a priority. Clients who may not be fully ready may recite reasons why regular meetings are difficult to schedule and focus on how busy they are. This is an important area to address in creating a coaching agreement with your client. Be assertive in your expectations for your client's accountability to make coaching meetings a priority. Mary Beth O'Neill, author of *Executive*

Coaching With Backbone and Heart (2000, 16), defines "backbone" as being able to state your views clearly. Be prepared to address what you need from the client to ensure a smooth process and to prevent misunderstandings.

Clients are ready for coaching when they show willingness and even eagerness for the coach to gather feedback data from co-workers about their effectiveness. If your clients are resistant to data gathering, inquire as to their reasons for the resistance. Address the concerns. In our experience, coaching clients occasionally did not want anyone knowing they had coaches. Again, what is the reasoning? What does having a coach mean to them? You may want to test the assumption that having a coach means being a failure and needing help. Additional lines of inquiry might be to discuss the consequences of not getting feedback from others and relying only on self-assessment.

In the case of Jennifer and Walter, it appears, at least on the surface, that Walter is open to Jennifer gathering feedback data from his colleagues. However, his comment that he expects only positive feedback may signal problems ahead. Would he be so eager if he suspected any constructive feedback? Would he be willing to change in response to constructive feedback? Is Walter willing to change any of his behaviors? If Jennifer had asked more skillful questions he might have uncovered the answers to these questions.

Ethical Conduct

The International Coach Federation (ICF) is a not-for-profit, individual membership organization formed by professionals worldwide who practice business and personal coaching. ICF has published a set of ethical standards that ICF members pledge to uphold. While the coaching profession is not licensed—as are clinical psychologists or social workers—the growing influence of ICF's standards on coaching practice indicates how much the coaching profession has grown and evolved. It is appropriate to review and even hand out a set of the ICF ethical standards as part of your conversation with your coaching client about your coaching agreement. Below are the major topics covered by the ICF standards, but the complete set of standards and guidelines may be found at www.coachfederation.org:

- ▶ Be an advocate for coaching.
- ▶ Be truthful in coaching claims.
- ▶ Honor others' coaching approaches.
- ▶ Be vigilant about misuses of coaching.

- ▶ Seek professional assistance as needed.
- ▶ Conduct coaching research with integrity.
- ▶ Honor confidentiality of clients' information.
- ▶ Set appropriate boundaries regarding physical contact.
- ▶ Do not engage in sexual contact.
- ▶ Construct clear agreements with clients.
- ▶ Identify coaching qualifications truthfully.
- ▶ Do not exploit coaching relationships for advantage.
- ▶ Respect the clients' right to terminate the relationship.
- ▶ Refer to other professional services as appropriate.
- ▶ Disclose conflicts of interest.

In Jennifer and Walter's conversation about their coaching relationship, a number of potential ethical issues could be problematic. Certainly, coaching could be misused in this organization, given the information the CEO shared with Jennifer. Jennifer was not vigilant about its possible misuse. Another red flag is the meeting location—the restaurant after working hours. Given the fact that Walter has been accused of sexual harassment, Jennifer should have set more appropriate boundaries. Also, if he has a drinking problem, perhaps Jennifer should have asked the CEO whether or not Walter is receiving professional help. And, obviously, Jennifer did not construct a clear agreement with Walter other than to collect data. Many aspects of a coaching agreement were left undiscussed.

Coaching Agreements

By now you probably realize that you should come to the first meeting with your prospective coaching client ready with a number of topics to discuss. Exactly right! Depending on whether you are an internal or external coach, you may need to construct a formal contract with your client following this meeting. The checklist in exhibit 3-1 provides topics you should cover in the coaching agreement conversation with your prospective client. Some examples for each checklist point are also noted. We encourage you to design your own coaching agreement format to fit the particular needs of your organization and clients.

This chapter addresses the elements needed to build a solid foundation for the coaching relationship. These elements should be considered in establishing the right fit between coach and client, determining the client's readiness for coaching, and applying guidelines for ethical conduct.

Exhibit 3-1. The Coaching Agreement Checklist.

✓ We will hold regular coaching meetings.
Example: We will hold meetings every two weeks beginning on May 1.

✓ We will hold a minimum of six coaching meetings beyond the data feedback meeting.
Example: After the data feedback meeting on May 31, we will hold six coaching meetings by August 31.

✓ We will communicate outside of coaching meetings using a combination of phone and email.
Example: Between regular face-to-face meetings, we will return one another's email and cell phone messages within 24 hours.

✓ We will use an agreed-upon protocol for postponing or canceling meetings.
Example: The client and coach will give 24-hours notice for postponing or canceling a coaching meeting for reasons other than a personal emergency.

✓ We will use an action plan format for documenting actions and progress.
Example: The client will be responsible for the agenda at each coaching meeting. The coach will document client progress at each meeting following the elements of the coaching action plan format discussed and agreed upon.

✓ The coaching partnership is based on the performance expectations of the coach and the client.
Example: The coach's performance expectations are to support the client in progressing toward achievement of coaching objectives in improved teamwork, organization, and interpersonal communication. The client's performance expectations are to achieve measurable results as documented in the coaching action plan toward improved teamwork, organization, and interpersonal communication.

✓ The coaching partnership will employ methods for measurement of results both before and after coaching.
Example: A 360-degree survey method will be used for both pre- and post-coaching data collection to measure behavior effectiveness of the coaching objectives.

✓ The coach will go beyond superficial talk to explore desired outcomes, fears, and feelings.
Example: The coaching conversation is a safe place for confidential dialogue. The coach will ask probing questions designed to inquire into the client's reasoning; test the client's assumptions; and surface beliefs, feelings, and ideas for action.

✓ The coach and client will set a protocol for handling problems in the coaching process.
Example: If the client or coach perceives any issue that affects adversely on the effectiveness of the coaching partnership, both parties agree to identify the issue for dialogue. If mutual dialogue does not satisfy the needs of both the client and the coach, they agree that the director of human resources may be consulted for further action.

✓ The coaching partnership is confidential.
Example: The coach follows the ICF Ethical Guidelines and provides a copy of these guidelines to the client. All coaching conversations are confidential except those conversation elements specifically agreed to by the client as not confidential.

✓ The client is ensured final decision making in choosing a coach.
Example: The client is given a slate of three potential coaches to interview and chooses the coach the client determines to be the best fit.

Moving Ideas to Action

Referring to the examples presented in exhibit 3-1, answer the questions in table 3-2 for your particular program planning. You can also answer these questions separately for each coaching partnership.

Table 3-2. My Coaching Agreement Checklist.

- How often will my client and I meet?
- How many coaching meetings will we hold?
- What commitment will I make to communication with my client between meetings?
- What will my policy and procedure be if my client cancels meetings?
- How will I document my client's actions and progress toward objectives?
- What are the performance expectations of me, the coach?
- What are the performance expectations of my client?
- The coaching partnership will employ which methods for measurement of results both before and after coaching?
- How will my client and I talk to each other?
- What will I do if problems arise?
- How will I ensure confidentiality?
- How will I give the client a voice in choosing a coach?

Co-Creating the Partnership

In this chapter, you'll learn

▶ how to create a safe coaching space between you and your client

▶ how to speak "the language of coaching" and how it differs from everyday workplace conversation

▶ the three levels of listening and techniques to perfect your listening approach

▶ the balance between inquiry and advocacy

▶ the top 10 dialogue techniques for successful coaching

Introduction: Raj's Case

Pamela is a new coach, and she is preparing for her next coaching meeting with Raj, a rather difficult manager. Raj has issues with control and micromanaging. Wanting a bit of assistance, Pamela approaches a more seasoned coach, Tyrone, and asks for some tips. Pamela knows that the use of dialogue techniques is paramount in guiding the coaching process, establishing trust, and creating a safe space for coaching to happen. Tyrone reminds Pamela to listen actively and ask powerful questions that will guide Raj toward self-discovery. Pamela jots down a few meaningful questions:

▶ What are your goals as a manager?

▶ How would you describe your management style?

▶ What do you gain by managing the way you do?

▶ What other methods or styles might you try when managing people?

▶ How would you feel if your boss was always looking over your shoulder? What kind of message would this indicate to you?

▶ What might happen if you delegated more work and empowered your staff to do more on their own?

Tyrone also suggested that Pamela help Raj step back and gain perspective of his situation. In this way, it might be easier for Raj to see a disconnect between what he wants to achieve versus what is actually happening. Pamela thought carefully about this. Raj believes that micromanaging is the best way to manage. Unfortunately, the actual results in his department are low morale and decreasing productivity. Pamela realizes that Raj is in a vicious cycle and has set up his own self-fulfilling prophecy: The more he micromanages, the more he gets what he doesn't want. Pamela decides she needs to help Raj paint a picture of an alternative way of going about his role and redefine his underlying beliefs and actions to achieve a more positive set of results.

Thankful for Tyrone's assistance, Pamela thinks through other dialogue techniques she can use. She decides to kick off the next meeting with Raj by putting his situation in context, reminding him that his dilemma is common among new managers, and pointing out that he has many skills he can build on to get closer to his goals. She plans to demonstrate support, yet raise thoughtful concerns about consequences and alternative actions. She also intends to tell the story of two managers from other organizations who had similar problems and how they were able to adopt more successful approaches. And lastly, she underlined Tyrone's key advice: Ask powerful questions!

Pamela's planning of the upcoming coaching meeting demonstrates a very important ingredient of successful coaching: You can't wing it and say whatever comes to mind! Choosing appropriate dialogue to create a supportive environment and guide the client toward growth takes thought and practice. In this scenario, Pamela concentrates on active listening, putting issues in context, asking powerful questions, and sensitively raising concerns. Such dialogue techniques make up the language of coaching and the major skill set that coaches need to practice to co-create a coaching partnership.

At all times, the individual, team, or organization being coached needs to feel supported and safe. This is best done through the use of dialogue skills that build trust, understanding, awareness, and self-discovery. If this is not established, feedback will fall on deaf ears and action planning will be merely a game that leads to inaction and no change. The entire coaching process pivots on the coach's expertise in saying and asking the right things, at the right time, in the right way. This requires expertise in a

Figure 4-1. Organizational Coaching Model.

Adapted from *The Organizational Coaching Model*, Bianco-Mathis, Nabors, and Roman (2007).

series of dialogue skills that must be practiced and honed. The result will be the creation of a coaching environment where clients feel safe enough to embark on a path of continuous improvement. Consequently, co-creating the partnership—dialogue that is continually practiced throughout the coaching relationship—is shown as a process step in figure 4-1.

So let's begin!

Coaching Space

Coaches create a space of exploration, learning, safety, and discovery based on intense dialogue. This differs from training or reading a book. Coaching is based on fostering an interpersonal space for reflection, questioning, enabling, authenticity, and insight.

To achieve a coaching space, coaches must communicate powerfully, help others create desired outcomes, and hold relationships based on honesty, acceptance, and accountability (Bianco-Mathis, Nabors, and Roman 2002). In our initial scenario, Pamela was focusing on making Raj feel comfortable so he could consider his own behavior without judgment and safely move toward alternative behaviors.

By fostering a safe coaching space, according to Hargrove (1995), you can

- make it possible for people to take action within areas where they are most stuck or ineffective
- transform people's views of themselves and help them move from stuck places to effective action
- help people act even when the outcome is uncertain
- assist individuals, teams, and organizations in letting go of the psychological investments in present belief systems and test assumptions
- create practice field assignments that are both challenging and supporting
- inspire people and help them recognize the previously unseen possibilities that lie embedded in their existing circumstances.

Perhaps the best way to experience this is to think of a time at work when you felt safe and supported. What was being said or done that contributed to those feelings? What results were you able to accomplish? What were the benefits of operating in this kind of environment? Now think about coaching someone. How can you create such a space with your coaching clients? What kinds of things might you say? This needs to be your goal for every coaching meeting. Practicing the techniques outlined in the rest of this chapter will help you achieve this goal.

The Language of Coaching

The language of coaching involves using powerful questions, getting behind the reasoning of others, listening intensely, and using dialogue tools that empower others to reflect and grow.

Getting familiar with and becoming proficient in the language of coaching requires the same practice and mindfulness as learning a foreign language. You see in your mind what you want to say in your native tongue, you transfer your thoughts to the comparable words in the foreign language, and you then force your brain to produce the newly patterned words. Over time, your brain makes the switch more quickly. With intense practice and immersion in the new language, your brain begins to think in the foreign language as easily as it does in your native tongue. This is the same mind rewiring that you need to master in learning and practicing dialogue techniques. The reason for this is that you must control your natural responses and respond in ways that best assist the individual, team, or organization you are coaching—not what you might want to say or would find yourself saying within a non-coaching situation. Even though you might want to express yourself in a certain way, that certain way might not foster growth or understanding for the client. In fact, you might foster just the opposite—defensiveness, fear, or anger. Consequently, you need to flip the switch in your brain and use a more appropriate dialogue approach.

To understand the concept of dialogue more fully, it is necessary to distinguish it from other forms of communication. Dialogue is different from discussion. As shown in table 4-1, dialogue supports a coaching environment, whereas discussion hinders it. When you are justifying or persuading—something done almost unconsciously—you are using labels, causing defensiveness, and blocking learning. This creates a zone of hostility, resistance, and miscommunication. In contrast, dialogue invites reciprocal understanding and a higher level of meaning. This leads to insight and more positive action.

Three main skill sets practiced within dialogue are listening, inquiry, and advocacy.

Listening

In their book *Co-Active Coaching*, Whitworth et al. describe three levels of listening that are commonly used in the world of coaching (1998). These levels go far beyond nonverbal behaviors.

The first level is *internal listening*. If you use this level when coaching, you will only listen in terms of your own experience and needs. You'll listen to the words to formulate your own opinion, give advice, or offer your own story. Such an approach does not foster a coaching space and uses discussion instead of dialogue. Here are some examples of this ineffective approach:

- ▶ "You shouldn't have done that. You should have just walked out of the meeting."
- ▶ "I can top that. Once, my boss told me to write my own performance appraisal, so I gave myself an outstanding."

The second level is *focused listening*. When you use this approach, you concentrate on the other person, listening to understand. You demonstrate listening through acknowledging, asking questions, clarifying, reflecting, probing, supporting, and

Table 4-1. Discussion versus Dialogue.

Discussion	Dialogue
A form of verbal communication based on justifying, defending assumptions, persuading, selling, and telling.	A form of verbal communication based on inquiring into assumptions, learning through inquiry and disclosure, and creating shared meanings.
Example: "Just go to your manager and tell her that she is not giving enough feedback on projects."	Example: "I understand what you mean about not giving you enough feedback. That must be very frustrating given that you want to do a good job. I'm wondering what would happen if you shared your concerns with your manager? How might you go about such a dialogue?"

problem solving. This better incorporates dialogue and more active listening. The focus is on the client, not you. Note the more positive effect of the following examples:

- "So, Mary, you feel upset because Joan left without helping you with the data input?"
- "Help me understand. You believe this was inappropriate because the director asked you to develop the report and not Tamika?"
- "I can understand why you might feel discounted when your boss left without commenting on your presentation. How else can you explain his behavior?"
- "Let me see if I understand the dynamics at play here. You believe that the report should be done immediately, and the accounting department believes it can wait until after the holidays. Is this correct?"
- "Interesting dilemma. What options do you see? Might there be a way to satisfy everyone's needs?"

The last level, *global listening,* is the most sophisticated and embodies the essence of coaching. It includes all of the elements of level two and adds the dimension of observing; stating observations; making analogies; using metaphors; making connections to other ideas and patterns within the situation; and noting subtle changes in the speaker's tone, attitude, or expressions. This adds richness to your observations and guides the client toward action. By noting patterns and connections, the coach can surface insights that clients have not been able to discover on their own. This, in turn, leads to more focused direction, actions, and change. Note the following examples:

- "I've noticed that your voice has gotten much lower when talking about that incident. Why is that so?"
- "Your reaction to this decision you have to make reminds me of a person on an elevator—the elevator has stopped at your floor, the doors have opened, you raise your foot to step out, then you freeze, unable to move forward. What do you think?"
- "I might be wrong here, but let me know what you think about this: It sounds like you are scared of John. Might that be true on some level?"

Like all methods and styles of communication, it is not helpful to use the same approach in every situation. With practice, you will learn how to mindfully choose and use different listening levels and techniques to balance your approach and effectiveness.

A good exercise that you can do is to engage in a coaching conversation where you, as the listener, ask only powerful questions. Do not allow yourself to make comments or share an idea or thought. Just stick to questions. This exercise should force you to listen more deeply and intently to the other person because you have to use the information you just heard to formulate your next question—instead of using that time to formulate your own comeback or answer.

Coaches who have tried this exercise explain that it is hard to do. They have to slow down their thinking, creatively design questions to carry the conversation toward meaningful action, concentrate on what is exactly being said or implied, and form questions that guide the clients toward their own insights instead of blurting them out. Clients who partake in this exercise claim that they feel really listened to, realize that the questions are meaningful and require a thoughtful response, and find themselves formulating insights on their own without being told or pushed.

Inquiry

The second skill set is inquiry. You just saw how listening includes the use of powerful questions. Then what is inquiry? Inquiry definitely involves the asking of questions—but with a specific purpose in mind. Inquiry requires that you communicate from a place of genuine curiosity. It involves the asking of questions to discover the reasoning behind what was done or said, before assuming. Some inquiry questions include the following:

- "How did you come to that conclusion?"
- "How do you see this situation?"
- "What information did you consider when you came to that conclusion?"
- "Help me understand your thinking here."

Advocacy

The last skill set, advocacy, works hand-in-hand with inquiry. The purpose of advocacy is to share your thoughts and make suggestions by explaining the reasoning behind them. Once you offer your ideas with reasoning, you then ask for input to test your reasoning and foster inclusion and partnership. The following are some advocacy comments along with inquiry questions:

- "I came to this conclusion because you told me you didn't want to do that kind of work. Have you now expanded your career goals so that you might consider this option?"
- "I'm making this assumption based on the fact that you want to improve your presentation skills. Will this opportunity allow that to happen, or is something else going on here?"
- "Given the way you just snapped at me when I offered you that piece of feedback, I'm assuming that this is a sensitive topic for you. Am I correct?"
- "I infer from your tone that you are angry about the incident with your colleague. Am I making an accurate inference?"

> ► "I see this as a situation where your department and the other department have conflicting goals. How do you see the situation?"
> ► "Let me share with you a possible approach. After you hear it, let me know if you think it might work for you."

The goal is to balance inquiry and advocacy. It is not always 50-50. You want to ask questions in such a way that you get to the reasoning behind an action or thought—yours or your client's. When you have a need to share a piece of information, concern, or alternative perspective, do so by explaining your reasoning and then inviting the client back into the conversation: *What do you think? What might happen if you tried this? How do my thoughts support what has already been said?* In this way, the conversation remains in dialogue and does not fall into discussion, telling, or judging. It is an ongoing partnership, leading to discovery and growth.

More Dialogue Techniques

As you master listening, inquiry, and advocacy, you will find yourself noticing and acquiring more and more tools. Ten further dialogue tools are offered in table 4-2. From this point forward, mastering dialogue needs to become a daily activity, just like practicing a new language. A fun practice exercise is to choose one new dialogue technique per week and continually use it throughout your work. In this way, you will train your brain and dialogue will eventually become your preferred way of speaking, not a conscious struggle.

Dialogue Practice

As pointed out earlier, you must practice dialogue as if it were a new language. Train your ear and hardwire your brain. Read through the following dialogue scenario. Read it aloud so you actually verbalize and hear the techniques being used. Note the effect each technique has on the coaching taking place.

Mary Andrews is a customer care advisor and internal coach. She is coaching Bob Wilson, a call center representative, in the claims loss taking unit. They are working on three goals for Bob: using more open-ended questions, expressing appreciation, and avoiding asking customers to repeat information. This is a transcript of their most recent meeting.

> **Mary:** Well, Bob, it looks like you are asking more open-ended questions during your calls. When I listened to six of your calls from last week, I noticed that you asked the caller an average of 10 questions per call compared to the four questions per call you had been averaging. [*points out positive behavior*]

Table 4-2. Dialogue Techniques.

Dialogue Techniques	Examples
1. Acknowledge first, then raise questions and concerns.	"You can certainly try that approach. It will allow you to practice speaking up more in meetings. There are a few concerns we should consider. Let me share them with you and see what you think."
2. Put the message in context. Provide perspective. Prepare the listener.	"I'm going to share some feedback that may come as a surprise to you. It is different than what you have heard before, and I think it bears listening to because it comes from your peers."
3. Give an example, tell a story, or use an analogy.	"Another approach you might use is something I saw being used in another department."
4. Put yourself in the other person's shoes.	"If I put myself in your shoes, I can see feeling a bit anxious right now."
5. Focus on the ultimate purpose.	"Given that we all have our own departmental agendas, let's try to focus on the best integrated solution."
6. Point out the positive, and explain why it is a positive.	"That is an excellent strategy to use. You will be showing your support and also making your own needs clear."
7. Help to paint a picture.	"That's an interesting plan for how to conduct the new program. Paint me a picture of how you would implement that."
8. Use a problem-solving approach.	"Though your personal preference differs with that of your boss, what are some options for meeting your mutual needs?"
9. Play devil's advocate.	"If I were to play devil's advocate, I could view that comment as more manipulative than helpful. Let me explain why."
10. Offer your ideas; don't demand them.	"Something you might think about is . . . "

Adapted from *The Dialogue Deck,* Bianco-Mathis, Nabors, and Roman (2007).

Bob: Thanks, Mary. I'm getting more comfortable with using those questions. The cards you gave me remind me to use the questions, and they help me to practice. [*uses a job aid to assist practicing new behaviors*]

Mary: Great. What progress are you making with your active listening and note taking? [*asks for specific examples and does not talk in generalities*]

Bob: To be honest, I'm not making the kind of progress I expected.

Mary: Oh? If I put myself in your shoes I can see where you might be a bit frustrated . . . and I think I hear that in your voice. Tell me more about that. [*empathizes and asks for reasoning*]

Bob: Yeah, you do. You know me. I want to see 100 percent across the board in my next technical assessment. I guess we should add patience to our list.

Mary: Let's focus on our overall goal and notice what you are already doing and the progress you've already made. In the four weeks we've been working together, you've incorporated more questions in each call. This is bringing you closer to those higher performance scores. What's happening with your active listening and note‑taking? What do you mean when you say you're not making the kind of progress you expected? [*focuses on overall goal, puts frustration in perspective by outlining progress, and asks for clarification and reasoning*]

Bob: Well, I've been taking notes like we discussed during my calls. Remember, we thought that might help me cut down on the questions I was asking my customers when they had already given me the information. But sometimes I still get confused between entering the information in the system and taking notes on my pad and talking to the customer. I'm having trouble keeping everything straight. I feel more confused, not less. [*uses another job aid—taking notes*]

Mary: It sounds like our technique of note taking isn't helping. Let's think about what else we might try? [*poses question to get client to think through possibilities—doesn't give answers*]

Bob: Like what?

Mary: That's what we're going to figure out. Think about a situation where you do a good job of listening and you accurately keep track of information provided. [*doesn't fall into the trap of providing an answer, but asks the client to think of another situation that might be helpful in this situation—an analogy, a transfer of skill sets from one situation to another*]

Bob: Hmmm . . . well, I do a lot of home improvement projects and sometimes I attend how-to classes. I do a good job of following the instructions and steps, and then I can recall them when I'm working on my own project.

Mary: Okay. Think back to the last class you attended. How were you able to keep track of what the instructor was saying? [*asks the client to paint a picture and specifically play out the actions*]

Bob: Well, I was interested in the content because I was going to use it. I was focused on what the instructor was saying; my mind was 100 percent on him and what I was learning. I wasn't distracted by my surroundings, and I wasn't worried about what I had to say next. I asked a few clarifying questions when I needed more detail. I guess that's about it. How does this help us with my clients?

Mary: Bob, you just painted a picture of you at your listening best. All we have to do is see how you can use those techniques and approaches in the call center. First, you said you were interested. How can you mentally get interested before each call? [*notes the pictures in the head so the client can duplicate those actions in a new situation and uses the related story so it can provide insight to the present situation*]

Bob: Well, my customers matter to me. I want to help them.

Mary: Okay. So how can you focus on that desire to serve your customers? [*encourages the client to come up with new actions and helpful tips that he can readily adopt and apply*]

Bob: Hmmm. I used to have a sticky note that said, "How can I serve you?" right in front of my station. I don't know where it went.

Mary: I wonder, could we make a new one? [*poses the idea as a question so the client makes the decision to act*]

Bob: Sure, I can do that.

Mary: Okay. Next, how can you focus on the caller 100 percent with no distractions? [*moves the thinking and brainstorming to the next step by posing another powerful question*]

Bob: Well, now that we're talking about this, I guess each call gives me the opportunity to learn what I need to know to help my customer. That should help me to pay attention.

Mary: Perfect. Let me ask, since you've been incorporating more questions into your conversations, how can that work for you in this process? [*encourages the client to use the techniques in coaching to on-the-job situations through a powerful question*]

Bob: If I'm focused on my customer, I don't have to worry about what I have to say next. The questions will guide us through the process. And, if I need more information, I can ask a clarifying question.

Mary: Excellent. It sounds like we have a new plan to try. What do you think? [*summarizes the progress by offering an insight and asking the client to respond to that insight*]

Bob: You're right. I'm excited. I never thought about the skills I use in real life being transferable to work. I think this can work.

Mary: Good. I think so, too. I'll be looking forward to our next meeting and your update. [*acknowledges agreement and a sense of moving forward*]

This chapter has demonstrated the language of coaching—dialogue. It is through listening, inquiry, and advocacy that you create a safe space for the client to learn, discover, and grow. Through intense practice—like hitting hundreds of tennis balls or spending hours at the piano—you can rewire your brain so active listening and powerful questions become natural and easy for you to use. When you engage your clients in true dialogue, they will be able to reflect, face their learning challenges, and reach higher levels of success.

Moving Ideas to Action

Through conscious practice, you can rewire your brain so that the dialogue tools come to mind more readily. You can begin by using the application job aid in table 4-3. Think of a past conversation or upcoming conversation you need to have. Using the examples from table 4-2 as a guide, develop your own examples to fit your chosen conversation. Then give it a try in real time!

Table 4-3. Dialogue Skills in My Conversations.

Dialogue Techniques	My Application Examples
1. Put yourself in the other person's shoes.	
2. Tell a story or use an analogy.	
3. Help to paint a picture.	
4. Play devil's advocate.	
5. Focus on the ultimate purpose.	

Collecting and Analyzing Coaching Data

··· **In this chapter, you'll learn** ···

▶ why collecting data is vital for coaching success

▶ the three primary sources for gathering data

▶ how to choose the right data-gathering tool for the job

▶ the importance of data analysis

▶ how to organize data to get the best results from your client

Introduction: Jocelyn's Case

Jocelyn is a long-tenured, senior director in a large association. Four months ago, she contacted a coach. During their initial meeting, Jocelyn explained that she wanted to focus on prioritizing her projects and balancing her time. She said that many people made demands of her and that she felt as though she wasn't meeting those demands as expected. One of the questions her coach asked her was what commitments or projects might she be willing to delegate or let go of for a time, to which Jocelyn replied, "Oh, there isn't anything I can give up." When her coach asked her, "What is the reward you are currently realizing for approaching your projects and commitments in the way you do?" Jocelyn was stumped. She said that she really didn't know and that she'd have to think about the answer. Although Jocelyn and her coach were supposed to meet two weeks later, they did not meet again for three months. Jocelyn's schedule prevented her from making the meetings as agreed.

When Jocelyn and her coach met next, Jocelyn shared that her boss had asked her what progress she was making in coaching. Jocelyn's boss told Jocelyn that she was concerned with her schedule, her attendance at meetings, and the way she was meeting or missing her deadlines. In response to a suggestion from her coach, Jocelyn agreed to complete a purpose statement exercise and a self-report on values. She also agreed that some data gathering would help her get a picture of how she was being experienced by others, and she selected several direct reports, peers, others, and her boss for her coach to speak with. Her coach spoke with everyone Jocelyn had on her list. The data revealed that people were conflicted about Jocelyn. On the one hand, they recognized that she had great knowledge and, if they could capture her attention, she was willing to share that knowledge and insight. Among Jocelyn's strengths, people noted the following:

- upside potential
- innate capability
- intelligence
- resourcefulness
- knowledge
- diligence.

On the other hand, she was frequently running to scheduled meetings, arriving late, seemingly distracted, and leaving early to get to yet another meeting. People wondered about that behavior. She seemed disorganized, chronically late, and out of control. They wondered which Jocelyn was going to show up at any given time. Among the areas to strengthen, people noted the following:

- manage time in such a way to meet deadlines, get to meetings on time, and eliminate chronic lateness
- make better judgments about her job duties so she did not end up doing something that was not really her job and not involve the people whose job it was
- prioritize her job duties so that everything would be completed
- eliminate the perception that she was in it for herself.

Jocelyn's coach decided to present the data she gathered in the two broad categories noted above. She used specific verbatim comments Jocelyn's raters shared with her as had been agreed by Jocelyn and her raters. Jocelyn listened to the feedback, and in the conversations that followed, she and her coach worked through the potential upside of re-evaluating her schedule and the potential downside of continuing the status quo. Her coach tested out several hypotheses and helped Jocelyn think through the messages in the feedback. She also shared (with Jocelyn's permission) her own observations and impressions based on their time working together.

Figure 5-1. Organizational Coaching Model.

CONTENT

Defining the Role

**Collecting and
Analyzing
Coaching Data**

Designing Goals and
Tracking Progress

Managing the
Coaching Program

PROCESS

Building the Foundation

Co-Creating the
Partnership

Feeding Back
Coaching Data

Conducting
Coaching
Meetings

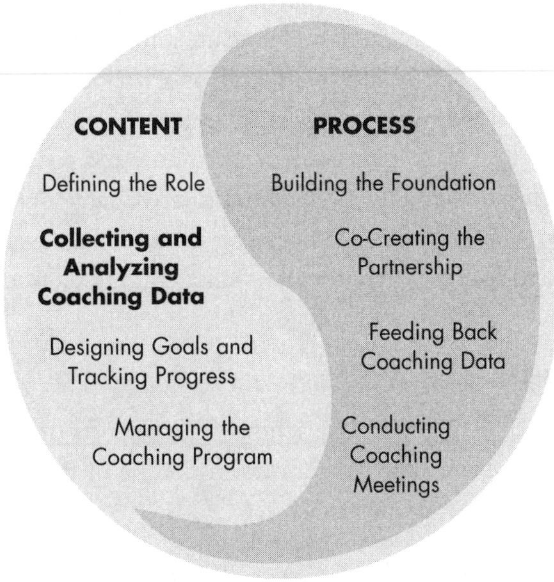

Adapted from *The Organizational Coaching Model*, Bianco-Mathis, Nabors, and Roman (2007).

Jocelyn's case reveals some of the opportunities and challenges in collecting and analyzing data. During their coaching conversations, Jocelyn's coach purposefully emphasized her strengths. As Marcus Buckingham describes in *Go Put Your Strengths to Work*, "the radical idea at the core of the strengths movement is that excellence is not the opposite of failure, and that, as such you will learn little about excellence from studying failure" (2007, 5). In other words, "a person or an organization will excel only by amplifying strengths, never by simply fixing weaknesses" (8).

The implication for coaching is substantial. Gathering data on strengths and successes and identifying winning strategies will provide the greatest leverage for growth and development. This is a departure from the more traditional approach, which includes looking at weaknesses. Depending on your clients and their organizations and the degree to which they have embraced the strengths movement, you will likely tailor your approach in gathering and formatting data. It is our experience that in the interests of full disclosure, the clients deserve to hear feedback on what is working as they intended and what is not. During the coaching process, you will be able to support clients in focusing and building on their existing strengths, help clients redirect behaviors that are not serving them, work with clients to develop desired skill areas, and help clients add skill sets and competencies. As shown in figure 5-1, this step in the model is presented as a content step because of its clear focus on data.

Typically, information is out there. The challenge is in capturing it and packaging it in such a way that it is of use to your clients. This chapter explores the sources and methods for gathering data at the individual, team, and organizational levels. The link among beliefs, behaviors, and results is explored as a way to frame data, manage cognitive dissonance, and guide change. Specific topics we will examine in this chapter include reasons to collect data, data sources, methods, and tools to use in collecting data; the pros and cons of qualitative versus quantitative data; logistical considerations in collecting data; considerations in analyzing data; and approaches to extracting themes from data and forming hypotheses when analyzing data.

Data Collection

Data are an integral part of effective coaching. The benefits of collecting data influence individuals, teams, and entire organizations. Some of the benefits of collecting and feeding back data include

- aligning intentions (clients') with perceptions (others')
- comparing the where we are with the where we want to be
- demonstrating openness and accountability
- supporting continuous learning
- helping create a high-performance culture.

When choosing a data source and method, it is important to think of the kind of data needed and how the data will be used. Once information is collected, it needs to be sorted into meaningful themes, which can be easily heard and understood by the receiver. Information is powerful when it is used as a way to seek continuous improvement.

Data can be collected from three primary sources.

First, you can collect information directly from your clients. This works whether the client is an individual, a team, or an organization. You can pose a series of questions and collect and analyze the answers. You can review documents that clients have created (for example, emails, reports, policies, meeting minutes). You can take a retrospective focus, analyzing past performance and behavior, and you can take a prospective focus, asking clients to define their desired results and identifying the necessary performance and behavior required to achieve those results. The inherent limitation of this data source (the clients) is the singular perspective they bring. Clients look at themselves, and others, through their own lens, which only represents a part of the picture. They may also have a vested interest in presenting themselves in the best possible light, and as a result they may color or shade information they share.

Second, you can collect information from others. Others may include co-workers, a boss, customers, direct reports, and family members. Others are anyone in addition to the client who is in a position to comment knowledgeably on the subject areas of focus. Others may have a concern about confidentiality and the intention of the data-gathering process. In addition, credibility, motivation, and intent have to be assessed and taken into consideration when collecting data from others. The benefit of others as a data source is that you are likely to collect many parts of the picture of

Dan's Case

Dan is a popular, likeable leader. As president of his organization, he likes to think of himself as being accessible and responsive to all employees. He tells everyone that he welcomes feedback. His senior team wonders, though, if that is really the case. On occasions when they have provided feedback, Dan has initially lashed out at them, and later, the person who provided the feedback is cut out of key conversations. Lately, Dan has been saying that he wants to make a shift to coaching leadership. As a first step, he wants to get feedback from each member of his senior team on what he does well and what he could do better. His team is uncomfortable with this idea.

In this case, Dan's credibility is not 100 percent. He will have some work to do to convince his team that his interest in feedback is genuine and they will not be at risk if they share their thinking with him. Sometimes people are very willing to share their thinking, and they are doing so for their own reasons.

Adapted from Bianco-Mathis, Nabors, and Roman, *Leading From the Inside Out*, 2002.

Sally's Case

Sally happily approached her boss's boss, John, with feedback about Marcia (her direct boss). "It's really hard for me to tell you this," she began and then went on to describe what she considered to be a critical problem with the way Marcia was handling a large customer complaint. As it happened, John was aware of the issue, and what Marcia was doing to resolve it. When John asked Sally if she had shared her thinking with Marcia, she said, "No, you know how hard it is to get time with Marcia, so I thought I'd better let you know what was going on." Luckily, John was aware that Sally felt she should have been promoted to Marcia's position and has not been happy since she was not selected. He asked Sally a number of questions designed to get her to think through her action in coming directly to him and the effect it might have on her relationship with Marcia. He also let her know that he would be speaking with Marcia and would ask her to circle back around and speak with Sally about her concerns. John encouraged Sally to initiate that conversation with Marcia. Sally said fine and left John's office decidedly less happy than when she had walked in.

In this case, Sally isn't looking out for Marcia or the company. Her feedback is intended to damage Marcia's reputation with her boss. Feedback will sometimes be positive and sometimes be negative. It is important to consider all data in a balanced way and to adjust the weight you give the data based on how and why they came into the mix.

the individual, team, or organization. The chances that you will gather a more complete picture are greater, and you can create the opportunity for your client to enroll these others in his or her future development and success. By including others in the data-gathering part of the coaching process, you introduce them to a role they might play going forward.

Third, you can collect information from yourself, the coach. In your work with individuals, teams, or organizations, you will have the opportunity to observe their behaviors and interact with them in a variety of settings over time. You can identify behaviors and patterns, note consistencies and inconsistencies, and as part of your agreement with the clients, you can bring this information to their attention. Through the use of skillful dialogue, you can inquire about your observations, test assumptions, and support your clients as they think through the implications of the data you have shared. As Mary Beth O'Neill describes in *Executive Coaching With Backbone and Heart*, it is likely that you will "notice a relationship between what the [client] talks about 'out there' and what actually happens in the moment between the two of you. When you notice this parallel occurrence, you can report your experience...and help your client get a clearer picture of what happens with her in her organization" (2000, 33).

Methods and Tools

Whether you choose only one of the data sources above or a combination of sources, you will want to use a data-gathering method or tool that supports your client's goals. Over time, you will likely collect a variety of tools that you have found work best in different circumstances. All tools have strengths and weaknesses. It is up to you to consider all of your options and to select the best tool for the job. Below you will find a discussion of six popular types of data-gathering tools and their strengths and weaknesses. Specific examples of these tools can be found in table 5-1.

Self-Assessment Inventories

Self-assessment inventories are popular and easy to use. Most are available in hardcopy or online versions, and they are generally inexpensive when compared with other data-gathering tools. In many cases, the clients have access to their results immediately. Many inventories are available in individual and team versions. Some self-assessment inventories are linked to substantive databases, which allow results to be compared with a general population norm or a specific management population. This approach provides a combination data source (self and others) because the clients are completing the assessment on themselves, and they are viewing their results against a larger database. Often this comparison provokes reflection and allows clients to consider where they fall on a given continuum and how they can leverage their strengths.

360-Degree Surveys

The 360-degree surveys are designed to provide individuals or teams with perspectives broader than their own. Most are available in hard-copy or online versions. The surveys have a unit cost that is typically higher than self-assessment products, and they may also require a set-up fee. However, 360-degree surveys provide very substantive feedback and a more complete picture than self-assessments. In addition to receiving their own ratings on a group of competencies or skills, individuals or teams can also receive data (including narrative comments) from the boss, superiors, peers, direct reports, clients, and family members. External administration may be required, and often deadlines have to be extended to allow a sufficient number of raters to respond. Many organizations use 360-degree surveys to support ongoing leadership development, and they publish aggregate results to show how the organizations are progressing on stated areas of interest. The 360-degree surveys can provide very rich, detailed data and are another combination data source.

Image Studies

Image studies are qualitative 360-degree surveys, designed to collect multifaceted pictures of individuals or teams. Interviews are conducted with colleagues, superiors, clients, direct reports, and other appropriate stakeholders for the purpose of identifying how the given individuals or teams are perceived and what their effects on others are. The data, once collected, are sorted into themes and then presented to the client. Verbatim comments (all of them or a representative sample) are frequently included. Image studies are best conducted by skilled coaches who can formulate targeted questions and then hold productive conversations with the selected raters.

Climate and Employee Opinion Surveys

Climate and employee opinion surveys are popular tools for taking the pulse of a department, a division, or an entire organization. Most frequently provided online, these surveys inquire about employees' satisfaction with a number of specified organization dimensions. They can provide valuable baseline data, are generally easy to use, and can measure progress as organizations work on specific areas. The risk with this tool as with others is in failing to act. If the employees perceive that their feedback isn't valued or acted upon, the organization's credibility can suffer.

Focus Groups

Focus groups have long been a popular method of gathering data on specific topics. They require skillful facilitation, and traditional focus groups also require compilation of data. They can provide real-time feedback on current topics of interest to the team or organization. In addition to traditional focus groups, there are many groupware and group systems products that allow you to collect data from individuals and

Table 5-1. Data Collection Methods.

Types	Examples	Strengths	Weaknesses
Self-Assessment Inventories	• Myers-Briggs Type Indicator (Briggs and Briggs-Myers 1998) • Co-Active Coaching (Whitworth et al. 1998) • CleanSweep (Leonard 1998) • The Career Architect (Lombardo and Eichinger 1992) • Emotional Competence Inventory (Boyatzis and Goleman 2001) • BarOn EQ-I (www.mhsassessments.com) • Strengths Finder (www.strengthsfinder.com) • VIA Signature Strengths Questionnaire (www.authentichappiness.com) • Thomas-Kilmann Conflict Mode Instrument (Thomas and Kilmann 1974, www.cpp.com)	• Affordable • Easy to use • Results are immediately available	• Offer only one perspective • Information may not be complete • May have too narrow of a focus
360-Degree Surveys	• Listing of vendors (www.hr-software.net) • BarOn EQ360 (www.mhsassessments.com) • Center for Creative Leadership, suite of 360 assessments (www.ccl.org) • FeedbackPlus, suite of 360 assessments (www.facilitatelearning.com)	• Comprehensive look from the various rater groups • Comparison of ratings between self and others • Large normative databases available • Can provide quantitative and qualitative data • Ratings must be interpreted • Follow-up coaching is advisable	• Administrative time can be demanding (solving technical problems, following up with raters) • Ratings can be inflated • Pricing is higher than self-assessments; requires adequate budget for 360 and follow-up • Ratings must be interpreted • Follow-up coaching is advisable
Image Studies	Data are collected by a trained coach who has the chance to ask follow-up questions of the raters. The coach comes away with the data and the impressions and perceptions shared by the raters.	• Obtains rich data with specific examples • Highlights any gap between what others are expecting and what the clients are experiencing • Directly controlled by the coach from interviews through feedback delivery	• Requires a trained, skilled coach • Requires expertise in qualitative data sorting • Not everyone feels comfortable with face-to-face interaction during the data-gathering process • Labor intensive to conduct personal interviews, sort data, and prepare feedback

Climate and Employee Opinion Surveys	• Customized products • GroupSystems (www.groupsystems.com) • SurveyMonkey (www.surveymonkey.com) • DecisionWise (www.decwise.com)	• Easy to administer • Respondents like providing data anonymously • Easy to re-administer • Provides ongoing measure	• Initial expense can be high • Requires internal coordination and reminders • Employees may expect action more quickly than is taken
Focus Groups	Data are collected by a facilitator using notes or electronic group systems tools. • GroupSystems (www.groupsystems.com)	• Participants can see, hear, and build on one another's points • Facilitator-designed and -led process • GroupSystems supports confidentiality and allows for flexibility in changing questions and formatting the collated product	• Participants may be reluctant to share experiences or perspectives • Possibility for group think to influence responses
Observation and Shadowing	A trained coach identifies with the client areas to observe and note. Depending on the agreement, the coach provides feedback in real time or after the fact.	• Yields powerful data observed by the coach • The coach experiences and can report on the client's behaviors and their effects • The coach can make space for the client to practice an alternative behavior in the moment	• Can be expensive and time intensive • Requires a trained coach • May be intrusive or distracting

preserve the confidentiality of the source. Following an agreed-upon protocol, people respond to questions using computers or keypads and the results are displayed in aggregate, as percentages, or specifically, with no attribution. Questions can be edited or changed in real time by the facilitator depending on the feedback or response from the group, and reports can be formatted in a variety of ways. These products offer the confidentiality of an online survey and the real-time feel of a focus group. The software also supports brainstorming, decision making, action planning, and consensus building.

Observation and Shadowing

Observation and shadowing are most often structured activities where coaches accompany clients as they go about their work activities. The opportunity to see your clients in action is substantial, and, depending on the agreement, coaches can provide real-time feedback on the behaviors they experience or they can provide feedback later in a planned coaching session. Some organizations may not welcome this type of data gathering, and not all clients are comfortable granting this level of access. A less structured example of observation can occur with the coach providing observations to the client during their coaching meetings.

Making a Choice

Given the wide range of data-gathering tools available, your final selection will likely be determined by the answers to the following questions.

What tools offer the best fit with your clients? In other words, what sort of data will the clients find credible? Do they or their organization prefer narrative or statistical data? What comfort level do they have with your direct access to data sources? What is their learning style, and what tool will best support it? *Fit* is defined by your clients and their organizations. You want to select a tool that will be meaningful and an approach that will support, not weaken, the coaching process.

What are the available resources? Specifically, how much time is available for data gathering and analysis? What is the budget for purchasing tools? What kind of time are raters willing and able to spend participating in the process? You want to select a tool that considers the resources you have to work with and will give you the best balance of depth and breadth in your data collection.

What is the intended use of the data? Of course, the primary purpose of gathering data is to provide your client with information to support action. In addition, what is the interest in resurveying the same raters at a later date? How important is it to provide pre- and post-coaching data? What is the benefit of using a tool that will allow a team composite report in addition to an individual report? As the coach, you want to select a tool that supports the measures of success outlined and is agreed-upon by your clients and your clients' organizations.

Consider the following scenarios, and apply the questions above. Where do your answers lead you? What data-gathering tools would you recommend in each case? Why?

1. Scenario: The employees in a program office have had six directors in six years. They complete an online survey annually and have indicated a lack of trust in senior management. In addition, communication, recognition, respect, and career development received negative ratings. The new director joined the office just following the most recent survey, and he is concerned with the ratings. He wants to get clarification on several content areas, and he wants to address the areas of most concern.

Answer: You may be thinking of electronic focus groups or one-on-one interviews as your preferred data-gathering tools. Both of those choices will allow you to ask clarifying questions and collect data while preserving confidentiality. There is also a personal dimension to those tools that may support the effort whereas another survey may not.

2. Scenario: An executive and her team of eight vice presidents want to know how they are perceived as the top team of the organization, specifically as related to aligned communications and decision making. They want to get detailed feedback on behaviors with specific examples so they can work on real changes. They are very numbers driven and want to have a baseline against which to assess their progress.

Answer: A 360-degree survey might suit the needs of the executive team by providing detailed feedback and a baseline of information from which they can build. Many 360 tools allow for verbatim comments, which can further detail what people are experiencing. In addition to the individual reports, many tools can also generate team reports so they can look at trends, strengths, and areas to develop as a team. Because they are numbers driven, they may trust a 360 with substantial quantitative content more than a tool that generates only qualitative data.

3. Scenario: A manager is experiencing a lot of resistance and complaints from her staff. She is very helpful to colleagues and is very responsive to her boss. She doesn't understand what is causing her to be ineffective with her staff. After all, she was one of them before she was recently promoted to her current position.

Answer: Your client may be facing a skill issue or an interpersonal or cultural issue since she has moved from being one of the team to being the boss. One-on-one interviews may provide multiple perspectives from her staff and allow for clarifying questions. You may also have the opportunity to paint a picture of the ways in which they might play a role going forward in supporting the boss and getting their needs met, if they are interested in so doing. In all cases, you will want to consider fit, resources, and intention to help you select the best possible data-gathering tools.

Data Analysis

Sorting through feedback data is analogous to writing a research paper. Imagine you are writing a paper on Abraham Lincoln. As you read documents, visit museums, and conduct interviews with various historians, you are collecting a large amount of information. To make sense out of all the data, you begin to sort and organize the data into related topics—birth and youth, schooling and first jobs, political career, years as president, and death and legacy. Then, you keep sorting through your notes, editing and refining it into a coordinated and well-worded paper. The same process is necessary when analyzing data for feedback.

Once data have been collected, it is the coach's job to sort the data so that clients can consider the information and see themselves as others do. It is important to keep an open mind as you collect, categorize, and link pieces of data. Taken separately, each piece of data reveals discrete information at given points in time. Collectively, data reveal themes, patterns, and inconsistencies that have to be worked through, analyzed, and presented to clients. It is critical to strike a balance of directness and care so that clients are energized, not paralyzed, by the information.

Let's look at an example of raw data, in exhibit 5-1, collected from three sources about the subject, Craig, a project manager with a well-known technology company. He completed a self-assessment focusing on emotional intelligence. Craig, his boss, four peers, and five direct reports completed a 360-degree feedback instrument. His coach conducted personal interviews with Craig's boss, three peers, and three direct reports.

It is difficult to read through all of these data points and distill them in such a way that encourages reflection and action. Let's consider the information on Craig by breaking it up into pieces, starting with the self-assessment. Craig received a low average overall score on this emotional intelligence instrument. Based on this, what are two working hypotheses you might create? One hypothesis may be that Craig hasn't had much coaching on or work to support his development in emotional intelligence. A second hypothesis may be that Craig doesn't have an interest in emotional intelligence. The important consideration at this point is to keep your hypotheses fluid. You don't know the whole story yet.

Now turn your attention to the 360-degree feedback. Consider the consistencies and inconsistencies in these data. What do you notice? Participative management is listed as "most important for success" by Craig's boss and his other raters. Yet, Craig did not

Exhibit 5-1. Craig's Data.

Data Source	Data
Self-Assessment	• Total EQ score is low average • Below average score on emotional self-awareness subscale • Above average score on general mood composite scale
360 Feedback	• Decisiveness is listed as "most important for success" by self • Participative management is listed as "most important for success" by boss and others • Participative management average score by others is 3.0; score by self is 4.0 (5 point scale)
Comments from Personal Interviews	• Craig keeps his eye on the big picture, gives us a focus, and gets us resources. • Craig supports his people. He expects a lot out of his folks, and he gets it. • Craig keeps his people in the loop. He has a real open-door policy. • Craig is unpredictable. One day you meet with him and he listens well, asking thought-provoking questions directly on point. The next time he's distracted, and you have to fight for his attention. • Craig wants things done his way. If you present an idea that is in line with his thinking, he agrees and praises you. If you present something different from what he envisioned, he makes you feel small. He can get very aggressive with his questioning, to the point of launching a verbal assault on you, your thinking process, and your overall competence. • Craig hires people with good technical skills. They don't have to play well with others if he respects their technical expertise. • Craig is content to let interpersonal conflicts simmer. He doesn't work proactively to resolve issues with colleagues. • Craig is a great tactical and strategic thinker. • Craig is very passionate about where we need to go. • When Craig gives us his word on something, it gets done. • Craig has a bias for action more than a bias for feelings. I like that. • Craig is very smart and capable. He can get past the smoke and mirrors to what really needs to be done. • Craig's approach is more direct than what we're used to around here.

select that skill set as most important. Instead, Craig selected decisiveness as most important for success. If someone believes decisiveness is most important for success, how might he or she behave? What questions does this information raise for you? What are two questions you'd like to have answered?

Finally, let's review the comments that were shared during the image study interviews. What are some of Craig's strengths? What do people admire about him? Where is he effective? What are some of the things getting in Craig's way? How do people experience Craig? What contributes to this?

You might choose to break the comments into two lists, as shown in exhibit 5-2: what Craig does well and what Craig could do better.

Exhibit 5-2. Preliminary Sort of Craig's Data.

What Craig Does Well	What Craig Could Do Better
Self-Assessment	**Self-Assessment**
• Craig's general mood scores are above average.	• Craig's scores on emotional self-awareness are below average.
360 Feedback	**360 Feedback**
• Craig acts decisively and considers that competency most important for success.	• Craig thinks he uses participative management more than others think he does.
Comments from Personal Interviews	**Comments from Personal Interviews**
• Craig keeps his eye on the big picture, gives us a focus, and gets us resources.	• Craig is unpredictable. One day you meet with him and he listens well, asking thought-provoking questions directly on point. The next time he's distracted, and you have to fight for his attention.
• Craig supports his people. He expects a lot out of his folks, and he gets it.	• Craig wants things done his way. If you present an idea that is in line with his thinking, he agrees and praises you. If you present something different from what he envisioned, he makes you feel small. He can get very aggressive with his questioning, to the point of launching a verbal assault on you, your thinking process, and your overall competence.
• Craig keeps his people in the loop. He has a real open-door policy.	
• Craig is a great tactical and strategic thinker.	
• Craig is very passionate about where we need to go.	
• When Craig gives us his word on something, it gets done.	
• Craig has a bias for action more than a bias for feelings. I like that.	• Craig hires people with good technical skills. They don't have to play well with others if he respects their technical expertise.
• Craig is very smart and capable. He can get past the smoke and mirrors to what really needs to be done.	• Craig is content to let interpersonal conflicts simmer. He doesn't work proactively to resolve issues with colleagues.
• Craig's approach is more direct than what we're used to around here.	• Craig's approach is more direct than what we're used to around here.

So, why not just give Craig one big list of the things he seems to do well and the things he could do better?

It is easier to process or absorb information when we can organize it in some way. As David Rock points out in *Quiet Leadership*, "the brain is a connection machine" (2006, 3). The brain prefers to take data and connect them to pre-existing maps. These maps provide context and allow us to reflect on the data as part of a bigger picture. In Craig's case, extracting what he does well and what he could do better might provide a workable basis for a conversation. Identifying themes in the data and sorting the data further to include hypotheses may create a richer conversation. Sorted data are easier to process and reduce the risk of overload. Whatever sort you use, you may choose to provide all of the verbatim comments, none of the verbatim comments, or selected verbatim comments to give depth to the themes you identify. Whatever you decide, it is important to be clear with your clients and the people providing feedback so that everyone involved knows how the information is going to be shared.

Another benefit of sorting data thematically is that the tendency to rebut or argue each point is substantially reduced. Themes are more powerful than singular examples. And, sorting the data increases the chances that Craig will be able to take action in specific areas. A second sort of Craig's data could look like exhibit 5-3.

What differences do you note between these two approaches to sorting Craig's data? How will these differences affect the feedback conversation you plan to have with Craig? The first data sort gives you two large topics to explore: what Craig does well and what he could do better. This might support a substantive conversation. The risk in using two such broad categories is that Craig may not be able to identify actionable areas. Or, if he does, it may be difficult to prioritize when so many are presented. Finally, the amount of data contained in the two categories is substantial. It is likely to cause overload and, in that case, Craig will be paralyzed, not energized to act on the feedback.

The second sort breaks the same data into more manageable chunks. It also presents the data with hypotheses, which Craig can accept, reject, or modify to help inform his thinking. Once the data are in pieces, Craig can fit and refit the information, getting progressively more comfortable with it. With his coach's help, he can note patterns, themes, and make connections, ultimately deciding on priorities and actions he will take.

During the feedback conversation you have with Craig, you will want to explore the relationship between Craig's behaviors and the results he is experiencing. Asking specific questions will help Craig focus on that link:

- ▶ How are people reacting to him?
- ▶ What behaviors are supporting him?
- ▶ What behaviors are getting in the way?
- ▶ Why did he decide to approach various situations the way he did?
- ▶ What led to the choices he made?
- ▶ What results does he want to experience?
- ▶ What has to change for him to get the results he desires?

As he responds to these and other questions, it is likely that Craig will reveal his thinking and the beliefs that led him to behave in certain ways, which in turn led to the results he is experiencing. Once he shares the beliefs that led to his behaviors, you can help him consider alternative beliefs and play out what behaviors would support them. The emphasis in this conversation should be future-focused. The work of

Exhibit 5-3. Secondary Sort of Craig's Data.

Themes and Hypotheses	Strengths	Areas to Develop
Relationships with Peers • Craig is goal oriented. • When Craig identifies a goal, he doesn't let anything stand in his way. • Craig doesn't notice or doesn't value the health of relationships with peers.	• When Craig gives us his word on something, it gets done. • Craig is very smart and capable. He can get past the smoke and mirrors to what really needs to be done. • Craig is very passionate about where we need to go. • Craig is a great tactical and strategic thinker.	• Craig is unpredictable. One day you meet with him and he listens well, asks thought-provoking questions directly on point. The next time he's distracted, and you have to fight for his attention. • Craig is content to let interpersonal conflicts simmer. He doesn't work proactively to resolve issues with colleagues.
Relationships with Direct Reports • Craig cares for his people. • Craig is accessible and shares information. • Craig sets high standards.	• Craig supports his people. He expects a lot out of his folks, and he gets it. • Craig keeps his people in the loop. He has a real open-door policy. • Craig keeps his eye on the big picture, gives us a focus, and gets us resources.	• Craig hires people with good technical skills. They don't have to play well with others if he respects their technical expertise.
Communication Skills • Craig is direct, and his style may confuse others.	• Craig's approach is more direct than what we're used to around here.	• Craig's approach is more direct than what we're used to around here.
Drive for Results • Craig focuses on results and may not notice his effect on others. • Craig's drive for results may be alienating others.	• Craig has a bias for action more than a bias for feelings. I like that. • Craig is very smart and capable. He can get past the smoke and mirrors to what really needs to be done. • Craig is very passionate about where we need to go. • Craig acts decisively and considers that competency most important for success.	• Craig wants things done his way. If you present an idea that is in line with his thinking, he agrees and praises you. If you present something different from what he envisioned, he makes you feel small. He can get very aggressive with his questioning, to the point of launching a verbal assault on you, your thinking process, and your overall competence. • Craig thinks he uses participative management more than others think he does. • Craig's score on emotional self-awareness is below average.

analyzing deeply rooted motivations and pathologies belongs in therapy, not coaching. It is important though in your role as coach that you support your client in connecting the dots between his or her thinking, behaviors, and results. In doing so, you support your client in developing critical thinking and the skills needed to analyze the link among beliefs, behaviors, and results and to make changes in them as needed.

As you work with your client's data, allow your thinking to diverge as you consider alternative perspectives and rationales. Continue to ask yourself questions as you frame and reframe the data you've collected. Challenge yourself to identify links and relationships between different data points. Construct and deconstruct the pictures of your clients so that when you review the data with them, you will be prepared to challenge their thinking in the same way.

This chapter describes three primary sources of data, reasons to collect data, and some methods and tools used to collect data, and it examines the purpose of analyzing and sorting data, extracting themes, and constructing hypotheses. In addition, the chapter examines the link between behaviors and results, which will be revisited in chapter 6 when we explore feeding back coaching data.

Moving Ideas to Action

You can use the information presented in this chapter to increase your choices for collecting and analyzing data. Incorporating additional methods and tools will help you to provide richer data for your clients and support them in making informed choices. Use the template in table 5-2 to identify specific things you will put into practice.

Table 5-2. Data Collection Questions.

1. What data do I collect?
- How is your client going to use the data?
- What kind of data will your client find credible (e.g., quantitative, qualitative)?

2. Where do I look?
- What data sources are likely to have the strongest effect on your client?
- What kind of access do you have (e.g., written documents, personal interviews, observations)?

3. How do I extract themes?
- What framework can I use to organize the data?
- What questions can I ask to support data sorting?
- What questions can I use to highlight the link between my client's behaviors and results?

6

Feeding Back Coaching Data

In this chapter, you'll learn

▶ how and why effective feedback can help your client

▶ the skill sets that support effective feedback

▶ examples of effective feedback techniques

Introduction: Ty's Case

Ty couldn't move past being angry. When his coach shared his 360 feedback with him, he was surprised to see that his self-ratings in building trust and strategic partnerships were significantly higher than the ratings he received from peers and direct reports. What he was really stuck on, though, were the verbatim comments that referenced his "steamroller" tactics. Part of him, actually most of him, wanted to reject the data. The only reason he wasn't doing that was his coach, Nancy.

When Ty and Nancy started working together three months ago, she told him it was her job to support him as he worked to achieve his goals. One of those goals was increasing his self-awareness. She promised to always give him the straight story and to ask him questions that would encourage him to consider things in different ways. She said, "I'm going to provoke your thinking." Right now he wished she'd be a bit less provocative.

However, it made a difference to have someone clearly in his corner no matter what the data said. In fact, Nancy always seemed to show a curiosity about decisions. Ty didn't get the feeling that he was being judged. Nancy just had a way of observing and then questioning his intentions. When she listened to him, it was as if she heard what

Figure 6-1. Organizational Coaching Model.

CONTENT

Defining the Role

Collecting and
Analyzing Coaching
Data

Designing Goals and
Tracking Progress

Managing the
Coaching Program

PROCESS

Building the Foundation

Co-Creating the
Partnership

**Feeding Back
Coaching Data**

Conducting
Coaching
Meetings

Adapted from *The Organizational Coaching Model*, Bianco-Mathis, Nabors, and Roman (2007).

he was saying and what he was thinking at the same time. She had this way of getting him to think about choices and consequences. She talked about managing the gap between perception and intention. And, even when he was looking at an area to improve, she showed him how to use his strengths to create a better outcome for himself.

So, now he had some questions to answer: "What does this feedback mean?" "How do I feel about it?" "What are my choices?" "How will they serve me?" "What are the likely consequences of those choices?" "How do I want to move forward?" Ty put his brain in gear and started to consider the questions. As he did, he remembered something Nancy told him early on: Coaching isn't for lightweights. That was for sure. Lucky for him, he had the interest, the drive, and a lot to build on. And, he had Nancy, his coach.

As Ty's case shows, when coaches are effective at feeding back coaching data they

▶ place data in context
▶ support reflection
▶ help their clients make new connections
▶ help their clients make informed choices.

Feeding back coaching data provides the opportunity for the coach to help the client explore meaning, generate alternative ideas and solutions, evaluate options, and take action. Because of the dynamic and critical nature of these interactions, this step in the model is presented as a process step, as shown in figure 6-1. In this chapter, we will examine the skill sets that support this step from that perspective.

Place Data in Context

It is important to frame data so that the client can consider it as part of the bigger picture. In other words, any piece of feedback is not the whole story. Rather, it is a snapshot, taken at a moment in time. It is the coach's job to help the client see how that moment in time is part of a pattern of behavior or may be an unusual occurrence. Context is made up of elements from the past, the present, and the future. Our past experiences often influence our current behavior.

Alan's Case

Alan is a skilled chief financial officer reporting directly to the chief executive officer of a large trade association. His current boss is forward-thinking and fair-minded, supporting continuous learning and accepting the mistakes that sometimes accompany that way of working. His previous boss was very different; he clung to the past, resisted change, and promoted a "blame rich" environment. Recently, Alan had the chance to promote a process change that would have streamlined the budgeting process and eliminated a substantial burden from his staff and other departments. He didn't support the change, and the feedback from his peers and his boss revealed their confusion about his choice. Further, he damaged his credibility and has people wondering if he is the right person for this job. When the topic came up in coaching, he shared his thinking. "You know what we say around here . . . you can't get into trouble for something you didn't do."

Alan's previous experience with a bad boss has left him afraid to step out and promote something new. He had no idea that his choice would affect the way he was seen by his boss or his peers. After all, he is protecting himself. Alan's mindset is part of the context within which he operates. He will need support in creating new linkages between beliefs and behaviors so that he can operate more effectively.

Present experiences also contribute to context. In chapter 5, you may recall that people experienced Craig as "more direct than what we're used to around here." There was no mention of anyone trying to talk to Craig about his behavior or of explaining the expectations held by Craig's peers and others. In this case, Craig is operating from his own set of norms, and his behaviors are confusing those around him. Craig is contributing to his present experiences every time he interacts with peers and others in his organization. Craig's peers and others are contributing to the present experiences by assuming what Craig intended in a given interaction and assigning meaning to the behavior without asking him for an explanation.

People frequently assume rather than ask. It saves time. It also allows us to balance our perception of what happened with the other person's intention without any verification. In this way, we get to write our own story and script all of the characters. This approach is not helpful in promoting clear communication and transparency in behavior. So, the degree to which peers and others are willing to ask questions and test assumptions influences the context within which data will be considered. Other influences on present context include

▶ business goals and objectives
▶ personal alliances and commitments
▶ accurate reading of the situation or circumstance
▶ accurate reading of personal decisions.

Alex's Case

Alex is the vice president of sales for a mid-sized consumer products company. She knows how to get things done in her organization, always exceeds her numbers, and is focused on moving up to a senior vice president slot. Although she was taught by a "take no prisoners" type of boss, she has been paying close attention to the president's messages during the past six months about the kind of workplace she wants to create and the kind of behaviors that will be rewarded. Alex wants that promotion, so she has modified her interactions with others to more closely align with the company's core values. Her recent 360 feedback reflects the changes she has made.

The desired future that an individual wants to experience also influences context. Alex's interest in a more senior position (future) influenced her and helped her change her behaviors (current). In Alan's case, a relationship with a bad boss (past) continues to influence him (current) and is affecting his future. Context is influenced by internal and external factors that may come from past, present, or desired future experiences. So, how does the coach support the client in reflecting on these factors and others?

Support Reflection

Sometimes, clients just need a few targeted questions to support their reflection on the feedback data. For example, in Ty's case, even as he was working through his feelings about his 360 feedback, he called to mind the questions his coach had posed to him in an earlier conversation:

▶ "What does this feedback mean?"
▶ "How do I feel about it?"
▶ "What are my choices?"
▶ "How will they serve me?"

▶ "What are the likely consequences of those choices?"

▶ "How do I want to move forward?"

Other questions that can provoke thinking and help a client reflect include the following:

▶ "What result do I want to achieve?"

▶ "How does this (behavior/performance) support my purpose?"

▶ "What can I do differently?"

▶ "What are the consequences of doing nothing?"

The reflection process is often where the greatest learning can take place, so encourage your clients to take their time. Often, a client may jump to one interpretation of the data, when the opposite interpretation is actually more accurate. To help your client consider alternative perspectives, the skill of reframing is necessary.

Melinda's Case

As they were reviewing her image study feedback, Rusty asked Melinda what she thought of the following comments from her team:

• Melinda always has an answer.
• Melinda keeps a close eye on us.
• Melinda checks on me regularly... usually before I have a chance to go to her as agreed.
• Melinda usually rewrites my status reports, so I just worry about providing the basics.

Melinda was happy to hear that her team considered her the answer person. She put a lot of time and energy into being there for them. She believed that it was her job to make sure they succeeded and to do the heavy lifting. Rusty asked her if there was another way to interpret their comments. "Describe the climate you are creating in the team," he asked. Through dialogue with Rusty, Melinda realized that she was micromanaging the team. In fact, although she considered them capable, she wasn't demonstrating that through her actions. Working with Rusty, she was able to create a development plan that allowed her to facilitate more and control less. She started asking more questions and allowing the team to work out the details of assignments once they were in agreement regarding what was needed. One year later, three members of her team had been promoted and Melinda had doubled the size of her team.

Source: Adapted from Bianco-Mathis, Nabors, and Roman, *Leading From the Inside Out*, 2002.

Reframing, or any type of reflection, requires interest and energy on the part of your client. You can help your client channel that energy into the process of making new connections.

Make New Connections

Recent research in fields including neuroscience, education, adult learning theory, and behavioral science reveals that "...it's not that difficult to bridge the gap between a thought and a habit" (Rock 2006, 24). The implication for coaching is substantial. As part of the coaching process, the coach helps the client build bridges so that thoughts can become habits. With the coach's support, the client has the "space" to consider new scripts, alternative behaviors, and different stories. They get to "rewrite" the endings to the many dramas in which they play a starring role. They can "try on" new behaviors and approaches and see how those changes affect the results they are interested in achieving. Rock, and others, suggests that there is a bigger benefit in "creating new wiring" (21) than in delving into the whys and wherefores of existing thinking. So, working through the feedback process creates the opportunity for the coach to promote this dialogue and to support clients as they consider changes in their thinking.

Consider the case below. A customer care advisor is acting as a coach for a direct sales representative, John. This coaching relationship is one that they both agreed would be beneficial for John at this time in his career. They are already into the coaching meeting and all preliminary topics have been discussed.

Customer Care Advisor: John, let's consider the data we have available to us and see what it tells us. You may remember that I was going to speak with your supervisor, listen to some of your calls, and study the technical assessments for the past three months.

Direct Sales Representative: Yes, I remember what we talked about. I told you when we first spoke that I could tell you what you were going to find out. You could have saved yourself a bunch of time.

Customer Care Advisor: Well, I appreciate your concern for my time, and I consider it well spent in gathering specific feedback that we can use.

Direct Sales Representative: I guess. I still believe I can give you an accurate picture of how others perceive me.

Customer Care Advisor: Since you bring it up, how do you think others perceive you?

Direct Sales Representative: I am practically an expert; I have experience in our direct and agency groups, and I started out in claims loss. I know all of our systems, and I have other experience in the insurance industry. I have consistently scored high in all areas of my technical assessments except those "woo-hoo" customer care elements.

Customer Care Advisor: Yes, you do have extensive knowledge in each of our service areas and in the industry overall. How frequently do other reps consult you with questions?

Direct Sales Representative: Well, not very often. People are jealous, you know, and they don't like to give credit where credit is due. I know the answers to pretty much every question they might ask—I've seen it all.

Customer Care Advisor: So, if they have this great resource—you—so readily available, what do you think stops them from taking advantage of you? Just the jealousy?

Direct Sales Representative: Yeah, I think it's the jealousy. They just don't want to get answers to their questions.

Customer Care Advisor: Okay, so to summarize, your co-workers are jealous of you and your experience. Even though you have a wide range of industry- and company-specific knowledge, they don't see you nor do they take advantage of you in the role of a valued resource? Is that correct?

Direct Sales Representative: That's it exactly.

Customer Care Advisor: Let's look more closely at that. Interestingly, that's not it exactly, at least from their perspective. Other people, including some of your clients describe you as "abrupt," "mechanical," and "distant." Your co-workers see you as "rigid" and "inflexible" and perceive that you are holding on to the "way things used to be." I wonder what might be contributing to these perceptions?

Direct Sales Representative: Who knows with that bunch?

Customer Care Advisor: Remember, we aren't just talking about your co-workers. Clients are experiencing you in some similar ways. I wonder how much of this is intentional on your part and how much is the accidental by-product of your focusing on the technical pieces of your work to the exclusion of the interpersonal pieces of your work—including those "woo-hoo" customer care elements?

Direct Sales Representative: Are you saying you want me to get a personality transplant and start being Mr. Congeniality with everyone?

Customer Care Advisor: No, I don't see any personality transplants in your future. I do see you as a valuable resource that is going largely unused because people don't see you as "open" or "approachable." How does that benefit you, the team, the company, or the clients? More important, how does that help you to achieve the goal you shared with me of raising the skills of your team members and increasing the capacity of the office?

Direct Sales Representative: Well, maybe not so much. But that's their choice to use me or not.

Customer Care Advisor: Yes, it is their choice. I wonder, what can you do to influence them to make another choice? How can you behave differently so you achieve a different result—a result that is more in line with your goal?

Direct Sales Representative: I'll have to think about it. It isn't easy for me to see myself in this kind of way. I have always drawn a connection between efficient, no-nonsense call handling and skillful service. People are calling with a problem or a question, and I've always thought it was my job to get them an answer and get them off the phone. I thought that is what they'd want. Based on what I'm hearing, they want more. It sounds like they want a connection. I can't believe I just said that. In one way, it makes sense—I suppose there is a value in my passing on what I know. And, if no one's asking me, that won't happen. I just have a hard time using some of that new language we talked about and gushing all of the time.

Customer Care Advisor: Okay, fair point. What if we continue to work on the language and hold off on the gushing requirement and see where it takes us?

Direct Sales Representative: I'm willing to give it a shot.

Customer Care Advisor: Good. Let's draft an action plan.

Table 6-1. Effective Feedback Techniques.

Effective Feedback Techniques	Examples
1. Put the feedback in context. Be accurate and well prepared.	"Jan, if you remember, you decided that the best way to get feedback on your management style was for me to conduct an image study and then to review that data with your Myers-Briggs Type Indicator results and your own self-assessment. So, what I have done . . . ."
2. Provide balance (both good performance and areas for improvement), and build on strengths.	"As you know, Bob, you have excellent decision-making skills. If we brainstorm for a few minutes, I believe we can come up with some ways you can use your decision-making expertise in improving your planning and organizing issues. Shall we give it a try?"
3. Describe information in a factual, objective, and behavioral manner.	"During that last meeting, I noticed that you interrupted other people without acknowledging what they were saying. Twice I heard you say what you felt needed to be done very forcefully, and I didn't hear you ask for the input of others on your statements. What kind of effect do you think these actions had on others in the group?"
4. Explore the client's behavior. Identify the client's intention, and compare it to the effect of the behavior. Explore consequences (of action or inaction) and alternatives.	"Let's look more closely at the behavior. What is your intention when you get angry like that in the middle of the hallway? What are you trying to express or achieve? What effect do you think your yelling has on others? What evidence do you have of that? What might happen if you continue this behavior? What other behaviors might get you closer to your intended outcomes?"
5. Point out trends and patterns.	"Sandy, I'm going to give you one illustrative example but not a long list. The reason for this is that I'd like to suggest that you pay attention to the pattern that keeps showing up in all of the interview data. Namely, folks don't feel you listen to their concerns."
6. Provide support in working through negative feedback.	"I know this piece of data may sound a bit harsh. If you consider it within the overall theme of your goals for decision making, you may see that you have several choices for how to use it to support your development."
7. Role model good feedback behaviors so the client can adopt appropriate techniques: summarizing, clarifying terms, discussing effect of changes, demonstrating concern, and acknowledging.	"Jose, I don't know if you noticed this, but I actually use the dialogue techniques with you that I've been suggesting you use with your own team. For example, the way I always ask you a series of questions before moving into action items is something you can also do during your weekly team meetings with your staff. What do you think?"
8. Stress the difference between perceptions and intention; reframe to explore different interpretations; describe the defensiveness you are observing, and explore the reasons behind it.	"I understand that as an executive team, it is tempting to dismiss data from the rest of the organization that you perceive as whining. I will be the first to admit that there is a certain amount of whining in some data. That said, I wonder what they intended when they brought up these concerns? The data is very consistent across all of the divisions. What reasons, besides whining, could be behind this serious concern about the performance management system?"

9. Point out the need to influence perceptions and not to resort to blame or "right versus wrong."	"It sounds like you have done a lot to cater to the needs of your customers, and they are still complaining about slow service. It really doesn't matter whether they are right or wrong—or whether you are right or wrong. What matters is that your customers perceive that your company provides slow service. So, what might be done about that?"
10. Advocate, inquire, and test assumptions.	"Your last answer didn't sound very convincing. How certain are you of your feelings concerning that piece of data?"
11. Ask questions and explore alternatives, even if the client agrees quickly.	"Well, Donna, I'm glad you understand this feedback so well and agree that modifying your delegation might be appropriate. What suggestions do you have for doing that? Let's get down to your daily actions and what you will start doing differently."

John's old connections have him equating swift, no-nonsense processing of problems and questions with desirable service. New connections, based on the feedback he is hearing, lead him to consider connecting with team members and clients in a way he hasn't done before. John and his coach can now create some new wiring that will support him in practicing and eventually internalizing new behaviors.

Make Informed Choices

In the example above, John was acting on old information. He chose to behave in a certain way because he believed it served his purpose. When his coach provided him with current data that showed that wasn't the case, John decided to consider an alternative. At this point, he is positioned to make an informed choice. Even if he decides to continue to act in the same way, he is now aware that his old behavior is not going to yield the results he said he wants. So, it is the coach's job to support clients in making informed choices. How do you do that?

Feeding back data to clients requires authenticity, telling the truth, sensitivity, and appropriate framing. There are specific feedback techniques that can support your efforts in providing information to clients in a direct and caring way. As you review the examples in table 6-1, note what language sounds familiar to you and what language presents an opportunity for skill building.

Practicing all of these techniques and making the language your own will strengthen your skills as a workplace learning and performance coach. As you increase your skills in feeding back coaching data, your clients will benefit from your ability to help them place data in context, support reflection through provocative questioning, help them make new connections, and help them make informed choices. These skills will be put to use as you work with your clients in designing goals and tracking action, topics that will be covered in the next chapter.

Moving Ideas to Action

 This chapter presents several techniques that will increase your effectiveness when feeding back coaching data. Using table 6-2, draft a script that will support your efforts to incorporate these techniques in your next feedback meeting.

Table 6-2. Applying Effective Feedback Techniques.

Feedback Techniques	My Application Examples
1. Put the feedback in context. (What is one new phrase or question I can use?)	
2. Reframe. (What will I say to support my client in looking at the data differently?)	
3. Provide balance and build on strengths. (Which strengths can I leverage?)	
4. Describe information in a factual, objective, and behavioral manner. (What meaning should I take from that behavior?)	
5. Compare the effect of the behavior with the client's intention, and explore consequences and alternatives. (What is likely to happen if I continue in this way?)	
6. Provide support in working through negative feedback. (How can we use this information?)	

Designing Goals and Tracking Progress

- ▶ why tracking progress is essential to the coaching process
- ▶ how to identify and write goals that support action
- ▶ how you and your client can incorporate goals into a functional coaching action plan
- ▶ useful measurement methods and techniques to assess your client's progress

Introduction: Matt's Case

Matt is working with his coach, Walt, to strengthen his employee-development skills. He has verbally committed to providing more feedback to his employees, and he and Walt have had a high-level conversation about what this will look like. When Walt suggests documenting Matt's intended actions in a written plan, Matt doesn't immediately embrace the idea. How does Walt support Matt in reframing his thinking about coaching action plans?

Walt: So, Matt, let's talk about the best coaching action plan format to document the actions you are going to take in support of your goal of improving your employee-development skills through more regular, specific feedback. The desired result of this, as I remember, is that you can readily access notes and observations that will support you in holding substantive performance feedback conversations with your team. Ultimately, your intention is to develop your folks so that they can head up teams of their own within the year. Is that right?

Matt: That's the goal I want to go after. I'm not sure I want to document what I'm planning to do though. We discussed how I learn best, and I thought I was clear about my preference for an unstructured, fluid approach.

Walt: Yes, you were very clear about that preference. Maybe the word *document* is throwing us off here. It is my experience that a coaching action plan will allow us to focus on exactly the approach you're looking for, so let me explain what I have in mind. You shared with me that you played football in school, right?

Matt: Yes, that's right.

Walt: Okay. I imagine when you started you had to learn a lot of things, things like the rules, signals and what they meant, how to read other players, and how to execute the different plays—running, catching the ball, and taking a tackle. I guess in the beginning it was a lot to remember?

Matt: It sure was.

Walt: So, what helped?

Matt: Well, the coach kept a play book. And, we had regular practices where we focused on specific skills. We reviewed game tapes and critiqued what we had done. Some of us would get together outside of the team practice sessions and run plays ourselves. And, there was a running list of our team and individual stats throughout the season.

Walt: Hmmm . . . so, initially it was a lot to remember and focus on, right? There were rules and the mechanics? What changed as you improved?

Matt: Well, once I got the fundamentals down, I could focus more on other things—strategies, alternative plays, and things like that. I think I see where you are going here.

Walt: The whole point of creating a coaching action plan is so that we can keep track of where you want to go, where you are starting out, and what "plays" you want to try along the way. As you practice, we can see which "plays" work best for you and why and then build on that. The plan can look any way you want it to. The only requirement is that we write it down.

Matt: Can we draw it on a chalkboard with Xs and Os?

Walt: As long as it works for you.

Matt: Just kidding, where do we start?

At its heart, the coaching process is fundamentally about change. Coaches are charged with supporting their clients as they work to develop, acquire, strengthen, learn, and grow. The coach helps the client integrate multiple sources of information and feedback, plan goals for performance, and thereby achieve agreed-upon results. Throughout the coaching meetings, coaches help clients explore new thoughts, beliefs, actions, and skills that will strengthen the clients' ability to take actions that will achieve their goals. Identifying and agreeing on specific goals allow the coach and the clients to concentrate their energies on desired results. The potential for positive results will be maximized if clear, measurable goals are created at the onset of the coaching relationship.

Typically, goals and desired results are documented in various forms, collectively referred to as action plans. Many people associate the term *action plan* with some sort of remedial performance effort. As we saw in Matt's case, some clients may resist documenting their efforts. For our purposes, consider an action plan to be a treasure map. As the coach, you are "there to take the client to places where they would not have gone alone" (Reynolds 2006, I:57). The action plan outlines the desired destination (goal/objective), the mode(s) of transportation you will be using (for example, meetings, field assignments, journaling), your provisions (resources), the potential hazards (barriers), and the signposts or milestones you want to take in along the way (measures/progress).

Unlike treasure hunting, coaching can yield rich deposits all along the way to the defined X marks the spot. Coaching action plans make it easier to mine the nuggets that present themselves throughout the process and are critical as they facilitate tracking progress. They serve as a tool to remind you and your client of where you started, what ground you have covered, and where you are headed. Coaching action plans offer several additional benefits to the client and the coach:

- ▶ Action plans document identified coaching goals.
- ▶ Action plans support ongoing dialogue regarding goals and expected outcomes.
- ▶ Action plans allow the client to prioritize and focus on areas of greatest interest.
- ▶ Action plans provide the basis for tracking progress.

Figure 7-1. Organizational Coaching Model.

Adapted from *The Organizational Coaching Model*, Bianco-Mathis, Nabors, and Roman (2007).

To create a coaching action plan of any type, you must first identify one or more coaching goals. In this chapter, we will look at the steps involved in identifying coaching goals, selecting from alternatives, writing goals that support action, incorporating goals into a coaching action plan format, using a coaching action plan as a tool that supports learning conversations, and tracking progress. In figure 7-1, this model component is highlighted on the content side. Goals, action plans, and tangible measures are content-laden tools that support the overall coaching process. Some clients are eager to document their goals and begin working toward them. Others aren't sold on the idea. In Matt's case, his coach likened the coaching action plan to another tool Matt had used with success in the past. In this way, Walt was able to work through Matt's resistance and enroll him in the idea of using a plan.

Identifying Coaching Goals

Many clients enter the coaching process with specific goals already identified. Goals may be identified by 1) the client, 2) the client's boss, 3) the client's organization, or 4) other sources. The goals clients wish to pursue will usually be directly related to feedback they have received. This feedback may be related to performance, interactions with colleagues, effectiveness with others, or ability to achieve expected results.

Whatever the feedback clients have received, coaches have the opportunity to help them consider, prioritize, and select the goals they are going to pursue. Fundamental questions for coaches to pose to clients at the beginning of the coaching process are "What result are you looking for?" "When we reach the end of our coaching relationship, what will have changed for you?" "What is it that you expect to achieve through coaching?"

This conversation will likely provide you with your first coaching opportunity as you work with your clients to state their desired goals in a positive way. Often clients phrase goals in the negative. They may use phrases like, "I want to be less adversarial" or "I want to have fewer misunderstandings." They may use what Teri-E Belf, author of *Coaching with Spirit* (2002), describes as "free from language," such as "free from stress" or "pain free." As Belf explains, "free from language describes an anchor to the past" (134). Stating goals using positive language helps the client focus on the future. "I want to be more collaborative" or "I want to communicate clearly and directly" are positive goal statements.

At this point, the coach can ask, "If you are more collaborative, what will change?" or "If you are communicating clearly and directly, what will be different?" These questions provoke the clients' thinking on the future state they are envisioning. Answering requires consideration of the desired result. Coaches want clients to paint as detailed a picture as possible of that desired result: "If I'm more collaborative, my peers will include me in strategy conversations and I'll be able to contribute to agreements and decisions before they are finalized" or "If I am communicating clearly and directly, my direct reports will have fewer questions and will be able to complete assignments as agreed."

Once coaches have a sense of what their clients want as their desired results, they should work with them to reality test. One way to do this is to quantify what they have described: "You say you want to be more collaborative...on a one to 10 scale, where one is low and 10 is high, how would you rate your collaborative skills?" "In the desired result you described, how would you rate yourself?" "Has there been a time when you operated at that level? Describe it to me."

Your intention is to reality test your client's stated goal. It is healthy to stretch when setting goals. It is also healthy to have a realistic view of what is possible in a set period of time. It is unlikely that someone will move from a 2 on the 1 to 10 scale to a 10 on the same scale without concentrated and prolonged effort. It is the coaches' job to help their clients set achievable and challenging goals.

Selecting from Alternatives

Sometimes, your clients will generate numerous goals of interest. Other times, they will identify one or two goals that are related to a key skill area. In either case, it is important to consider current circumstances and help clients identify the goals they will focus on first. In making this selection, coaches should consider a number of factors:

- ▶ What strengths do the clients have to build on?
- ▶ What goal requires using those strengths?
- ▶ What are the consequences of taking no action? (Sometimes clients do not realize that choosing not to act is in fact a choice. To be fully informed, it is important for you to make this clear.)
- ▶ What are the pros and cons of each alternative? (Consider this for both the client and the organization. As the coach, you can help clients think through their choices within the context of their environment. The coaching process allows you to help your clients consider different perspectives by reframing the data they have available and looking at the data through a variety of lenses.)
- ▶ What opportunities are there for any quick wins? (Change is hard work, and it requires a lot of energy. If there is anything that your client can start or stop that will be visible and have an immediate effect, it will have an energizing effect and may lead to positive reinforcement from others.)

Writing SMART Goals That Support Action

The conversation thus far has covered what the clients want to achieve and what will be different when they achieve it. The coach and the client have generated a list of possible alternatives, and from that list the client has selected one, two, or three alternatives to pursue. While the possibilities for action may be limitless, the clients' energy is not. Coaches should help the clients focus on a specific area and sequence the other goals behind it. For coaching purposes, a steady, purposeful effort in one direction will yield more successful, tangible results than a number of efforts in several directions.

Writing meaningful objectives is a topic discussed within many disciplines. The SMART acronym is one of the more standard approaches used in writing objectives and goals. Coaches can support their clients' efforts by helping them write their goals using the SMART formula:

- specific
- measurable
- agreed-upon
- realistic
- time-bound.

Table 7-1 shows examples of typical coaching goals and how the SMART model can be used to create measurable coaching objectives. Note that the specific format doesn't matter as long as the components are clearly stated and understood.

Incorporating Goals into a Coaching Action Plan

Once the clients have decided on the specific goal or objective they are going to work toward, it is time to select from a range of possible actions that might be taken. These actions will also be documented in the coaching action plan. Below is a list of possible actions a coaching client might take. Of course, actions must be appropriate to the goal or objective being pursued, but generic possibilities include the following:

- Journaling: keeping a running journal on actions taken, what went well, what didn't go well, what was learned
- Assignments: conversing, conducting interviews, presenting, role playing
- Feedback: getting a buddy to observe you at a designated event and give you feedback on your effectiveness
- Reading: books, articles, websites

▶ Skills practice: slowly practicing an activity by taking baby steps (for example, for improved presentation skills, giving a small presentation in front of four or five people, then progressing to bigger groups)

▶ Props: taking a notebook to every meeting to take notes, instead of speaking out like you normally do; keeping a pair of eyeglasses in your hands as you talk to remind yourself to look beyond your own narrow view in discussions

▶ Information gathering: gathering information on a need or asking for assistance

▶ Research: conducting a benchmark study to establish goals and how-to ideas from those who may have a better perspective

▶ Role models: observing others demonstrating something.

Once coaches and clients have selected specific actions in support of their identified goals, coaches will want to choose a coaching action plan format. There are many choices available for documenting coaching goals. SMART objectives can be deconstructed into actions and dates for a simple, uncluttered coaching action plan such as the one in exhibit 7-1.

Table 7-1. Coaching Goals and Objectives.

Coaching Goals	Measurable Objectives Using the SMART Model
1. Improve presentation skills.	Apply a proven and organizationally accepted model for effective presentation at the next board of directors meeting in July that results in favorable evaluations by a majority of the board members.
2. Communicate with other department managers.	Meet once a month with each department manager to give and receive feedback on agreed-upon performance improvement measures for joint initiatives recorded during each month, starting in September.
3. Demonstrate better teamwork.	Ask at least three more questions than I have in the past at regular staff biweekly meetings to determine ideas, reasoning, and viewpoints of team members, starting at the next staff meeting.
4. Improve accountability among department managers.	Request that all department managers who report to me use an action planning method to state objectives, actions, and due dates; track and monitor progress during biweekly meetings; dialogue about the status of the action plans and how I can support them. Ensure that we are on top of all aspects of performance well in advance of the next performance appraisal.

Exhibit 7-1. Abbreviated Action Plan.

Goal: I will create a personal elevator speech that allows me to effectively describe the value I add to any potential mentor or boss.

Action Items	Deadlines
Identify my top three strengths.	October 10
Write short examples of how I have used each strength to solve a problem or contribute to a desired result. Also, identify what makes me unique with this strength. What is my value proposition?	October 17
Practice my delivery prior to my first coaching call.	October 22
Share my elevator speech with my coach and solicit feedback.	October 29
Interview with potential mentors and bosses, using the elevator speech and assessing its effect.	November 12
Report results during my second coaching call, including effect in other areas.	November 12
Focus on strengths and value I add on a day-to-day basis, and report effect during third coaching call.	December 3

In addition to this simple format, there are other formats that are progressively more complex. At a minimum, whatever coaching action plan format you and your client select, it must be in writing. If you are wondering what a written plan provides, consider the following:

▶ A written plan captures the client's thinking and commitment at a specific point in time.

▶ A basic plan will include a timeframe and specific actions to be taken.

▶ When the client and coach meet, a written plan is one data point. The coach and the client can discuss actions taken, successes realized, actions not taken, and consequences. Most important, coaches can facilitate a conversation aimed at discovering what strategies support the clients in achieving their goals. How are they able to take action? What gets in their way? How might they have to adapt their plans to ensure their success?

This conversation supports clients in discovering what they need (for example, systems, processes, resources, support) to successfully achieve goals. This is a valuable learning experience that can be applied well after the coaching process is complete. A basic written coaching action plan might look like one of the two examples in table 7-2.

Table 7-2. Coaching Action Plan Samples.

Sample 1

Goal Statement:

Action #1:	Date:
Action #2:	Date:
Action #3:	Date:

Sample 2

From _____ (date) to _____ (date):

Goal Area #1:	Specific Action
Goal Area #2:	Specific Action
Goal Area #3:	Specific Action

These basic formats meet the SMART criteria. They include a specific goal or objective statement and actions that are measurable, agreed-upon, realistic, and time-bound. More substantive plans can include sections for detailing the results achieved and any reflection on the process. They may look more like exhibit 7-2.

Alternatively, you may have a client who is better served with more of a mindmap approach to action planning. The suggested elements are the same, but the format and presentation look substantially different, as shown in figure 7-2.

It is important to remember that the coaching action plan, in whatever format, is a tool supporting the coaching process. Your job as the coach is to use that tool to promote and support your client's learning, insight, development, and achievement. As you move in that direction, you will want to record your client's movement and track progress along the way.

Tracking Progress

You have worked closely with your client to establish goals and develop meaningful action plans. You learned important skills and approaches for helping your coaching client design and take effective action toward measurable goals. Measuring and tracking results is an ongoing process from the beginning to the end of the coaching relationship. It is important to apply different methods of documenting, measuring, and tracking the client's progress toward the achievement of those coaching goals.

Exhibit 7-2. Detailed Action Plan.

Goals or Objectives	Tactics	Date	Status	Performance Measures	Accomplishments
1. Increase effectiveness of membership database and online registration process.	1.1. Make online registration fully functional for all states and advisers.	1.1. May 15	(To be filled out for status sessions/meetings either one-on-one or in groups)	1.1. Online registration fully functional	1.1. Online registration fully functional in all states but Hawaii. Issue on its end, not ours. Will be remedied by June.
	1.2. Promote online registration in all publications, email blasts, and national briefings (keep tracking chart).	1.2. September through December (see attached tracking chart)		1.2. Online registration promoted within all cited situations (see tracking chart)	1.2. Online registration promoted through all publications, emails, and national briefings (see attached).
	1.3. Offer online registration sessions.	1.3. July and November		1.3. Online registration offered	1.3. Online registration offered.
	1.4. Forge strong relationship with employees to ensure best possible customer service from them (two conference calls).	1.4. By March 30		1.4. Strong relationship forged with employees as proven through follow-up survey	1.4. Strong relationship forged with employees (see results of survey attached).
	1.5. Educate staff on usefulness of database (separate meeting).	1.5. By March 30		1.5. Staff educated and using database, as noted on tracking chart (see attached)	1.5. Staff educated and using database (see attached).
2. Produce a live stream awards video.	......	......	......	......	......

Figure 7-2. Mindmap Action Plan.

Actions to take between October 14 and October 28

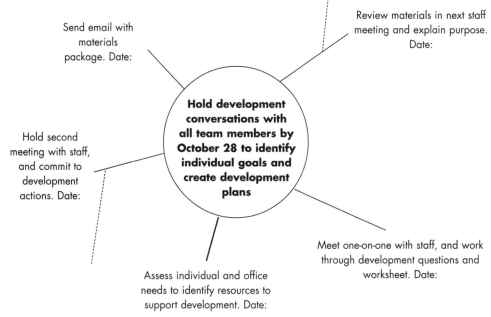

The action plan is a document that should be used to monitor progress, celebrate benchmark steps, add further notes and helpful mechanisms, and note special tasks to move through difficult transitions. The action plan should be the working document between you and your client as you progress from meeting to meeting.

Human nature will cause clients to revert to long-established behaviors—no matter how disruptive—when experiencing stress, frustration, health problems, pressure from upper management, loss of confidence, business downturns, or general life pressures. It is also human nature to make assumptions about how we are doing. People often label their efforts as either overly positive or overly negative without testing those assumptions. That is why the entire coaching process includes data gathering and assessment.

Given this, and given the fact that we are attempting to add new behaviors "over" long-established mental circuits (Rock 2006, 19-20), it is paramount to build in constant aids for staying on track. This is why there are established group activities and checkpoints like weight-loss weigh-ins, Alcoholics Anonymous meetings, and interim grade reports. Creating such aids for staying on track is also necessary during the coaching process. A measurement infrastructure supports the client as he or she works to incorporate new behaviors.

Larry's Case

Larry was puzzled. He had worked so hard, and he didn't know why things were going wrong. Six months ago, after receiving some feedback, Larry decided to work on improving his relationships with executives and managers across the three divisions within his agency. Larry had been told that he tended to act and think within his own silo. Folks felt he mostly defended and supported his own agenda within his own division, as opposed to taking a broader approach. He was told that it would be more helpful if he could demonstrate how his concerns and ideas benefited the entire organization, not just his own division.

Larry began speaking up in meetings and saying things like, "I have an idea, and I'd like to know how it will affect each one of your areas—and how we can make it a win-win situation." In staff meetings with his own immediate team, he emphasized the need to cooperate with other areas, think globally, and try to solve problems across all divisions and branches.

About four weeks later, Larry asked a few of his colleagues and direct reports if they had noted any changes in his behavior. One person said, "Well, you know, Larry, I think you have been pretty positive lately. That has been good." Larry pushed for more specifics, but couldn't get anything. One of his staff members said, "Well, yes, I guess you have been acting like you care about the entire agency. You have made some inclusive statements. But let's face it, Larry, you really are only interested in pushing our own area. You know as well as I do that if I'm faced with a decision that might help another division—but would hurt us in the process—that you expect me to play hardball. That's what you taught me and many others on the team to do for some time now." Larry didn't know what to say. He was stunned with the directness and truth in the feedback, and he was also disappointed that his recent efforts were not viewed as genuine.

Larry decided to talk to Juan, an internal coach. Juan assisted Larry in designing a list of visible behaviors and actions that demonstrated the goal of "cross-functional cooperation, support, attitude, and involvement." Juan designed a short survey on an index card, which included each visible action, a scale of one (not demonstrated) to five (demonstrated), and space for short comments. Then Juan had Larry come up with a list of five colleagues with whom he interacts several times per week who would be in positions to comment on Larry's behaviors. Juan and Larry then role-played how Larry could ask each colleague to "join him in his work to improve cross-functional interactions" by taking notes over a period of three weeks and then sitting down and giving straight feedback to Larry. Juan pointed out that this would be a powerful coaching technique for the following reasons:

- Given that Larry would know that he was being measured, he would be more mindful. This real-time observation process would provide Larry with a constant incentive to practice the behaviors he was trying to master.

- The process would be a demonstration of cross-functional support because Larry would be including others in his development process.

- Larry would be encouraging others to partner with him in achieving his goal. Therefore, the index card technique would force Larry's partners to look for new behaviors, not concentrate on every time he slipped.

At first, Larry wasn't sure he wanted to do this. He confided that this made him feel vulnerable and like less of a leader. Juan agreed that the process probably felt uncomfortable. He pointed out that having to live with the present perception of "only being concerned about your own agenda" probably also jeopardized Larry's future as a leader. Juan further explained that it takes not only practice and time to consistently demonstrate new actions, but also a long time for our environments to see us differently. Juan said, "Let's face it, Larry. Your colleagues have worked with you for quite awhile. They have already slotted you and labeled you as a certain kind of person and leader. It takes effort to change that perception, and it often takes more than your demonstrating alternative behaviors—they too must make a decision to give you a chance and actually notice the new behaviors. Engaging your environment to take part in the change process completes this circle."

Engaging people in the environment of your client in the coaching process is a valuable tool that supports achieving coaching goals.

Using Measurement Methods and Approaches

There are three important aspects of measuring results in coaching. The first two aspects have already been discussed: establish measurable objectives at the onset of the coaching relationship and collect performance and feedback data early in the coaching relationship so clients are able to measure where they currently stand in relation to those measurable objectives. The third step is the need for additional and repeated collection of performance and feedback data during and at the conclusion of the coaching relationship so clients can meaningfully measure progress.

There are several approaches to use for measuring pre- and post-coaching results. These action planning and tracking approaches will vary according to the level of coaching (individual, team, or organization) and may include strategies to address more than one level. The chart on measurement methods in table 7-3 duplicates many of the same methods outlined in chapter 5. This is to be expected since you may use some of the same measurement methods throughout the coaching process.

Choosing Measurement Tools

The next few pages include samples of five specific tools you can use to collect useful feedback midway and near the end of a coaching relationship. These tools should be tailored to your own coaching situations. The following tools are covered:

- ▶ quantitative gap analysis
- ▶ mini-feedback survey
- ▶ direct observation feedback
- ▶ self-assessment
- ▶ action plan self-evaluation.

Table 7-3. Measurement Methods.

Levels of Measurement	Self-Assessments	Feedback from Others	Performance Data
Self	• Quantitative gap analysis • Progress report • Off-the-shelf self-assessment	• 360 survey • Interview • Dialogue • Direct observation • Support network • Progress report	• Formal/informal performance evaluation • Progress report • Career progress
Team	• Climate survey • Dialogue	• Feedback questionnaire • Dialogue session	• Retention/turnover report • Team performance evaluation • Progress report
Organization	• Climate survey • Interview • Focus group	• Customer feedback • Stakeholder feedback	• Organizational performance assessment: —Audit —Financial performance —Retention/turnover analysis —Revenue/profit report —Quality assessment —Progress report

Quantitative Gap Analysis

This tool is useful for measuring results of coaching and can be adapted for tracking individuals, teams, and organizations. As shown in table 7-4, it is a self-assessment that can be used during the coaching process to provide a quantifiable measure of change. A client's own attitude provides the necessary mental push to consistently practice and master new behaviors.

Table 7-4. Quantitative Gap Analysis.

Top Four Challenges and Corresponding Coaching Goals/Behaviors	As I See Myself on a Scale of 1 to 10 in January	As I'd Like to See Myself on a Scale of 1 to 10 in September	As I See Myself on a Scale of 1 to 10 in September
Demonstrates patience	3	7	5
Listens actively	2	9	9
Offers suggestions without dictating	4	6	5
Encourages participation	5	9	8

Mini-Feedback Survey

A coaching client can use a survey, as shown in exhibit 7-3, to collect feedback from others on coaching progress. This can be used as a pre- and post-coaching tool to gather quantifiable feedback data from others and is useful in building awareness for individual behavior change. The mini-feedback survey has the benefit of engaging the environment so the chances for successful change—and acceptance of that change— are more probable.

The client should approach several colleagues and say something like, "Three months ago, I received valuable information about my team interactions. Based on the information, I decided to focus on three things. Please consider my behavior during the past 90 days and indicate what progress I have made on the −3 to +3 scale. Thank you in advance for your feedback."

Direct Observation Feedback

The direct observation feedback checklist, as shown in exhibit 7-4, is the most useful tool in involving others in the client's behavior change. By involving others, the client creates a community effort, and the culture is more likely to notice and accept changes.

The client should approach several colleagues and say something like, "Over the next month, I am going to be working on changing some behaviors. I would appreciate your help. If you agree, you can support me by keeping this chart visible and taking notes as you observe my efforts. At the end of the month, I will sit down with you to review my progress. What do you think?"

Exhibit 7-3. Mini-Feedback Survey.

1. **I ask questions to ensure complete understanding of feedback.**

   −3   −2   −1   0   +1   +2   +3

2. **I paraphrase feedback to check for understanding.**

   −3   −2   −1   0   +1   +2   +3

3. **I maintain an even tone of voice when responding to feedback.**

   −3   −2   −1   0   +1   +2   +3

Exhibit 7-4. Direct Observation Feedback.

Behavior	January 10	January 17	January 24	January 31	February 7
Is open to new ideas					
Clarifies who will do what and when					
Encourages open discussion					
Ensures participants equal air time					
Clarifies actions to be taken					
Reviews quality criteria					
Reviews customer care feedback					

Self-Assessment

The self-assessment, as shown in exhibit 7-5, can be used with individuals or teams to reflect on coaching results. You can use this during a coaching meeting as you review what was practiced or observed during the last coaching interval, or you can ask the clients to review these questions for each practice item and be ready to address specific actions they intend to take based on their assessments. Such a list acts as a monitoring tool and leads to aligning, modifying, and adding new behaviors to practice during the next phase of the coaching.

Exhibit 7-5. Behavior Self-Assessment.

1. Are you practicing the new behavior(s)?

2. If so, how often?

3. Who is noticing the new behavior(s)?

4. How do you know?

5. How does this compare with the results you intended?

6. What is your reaction to this result?

7. What obstacles (if any) are you experiencing in applying the new behavior(s)?

8. What new approaches or ideas do you have based on this experience?

9. Describe any additional support you require.

Action Plan Self-Evaluation

The action plan self-evaluation, as shown in exhibit 7-6, can be used to assess and discuss the results of a client's coaching action plans.

Exhibit 7-6. Direct Observation Feedback.

1. Were my actions completed on time?

2. What percentage of completion was achieved?

3. If an action was not completed, do I still intend to accomplish it?

4. If the action was not completed, what prevented its accomplishment?

5. What did I do differently from what I had planned? Why?

6. What benefits did the completed activity produce?

7. If I were to do it again, how would I do it differently?

8. What do I plan to do now?

9. If an action was completed, what is my degree of satisfaction with the outcome?

10. Who will benefit the most from this action?

11. Specifically, what was improved as a result of the activity?

12. What money was saved or what value was added to the organization as a result of the action?

13. What did I, my team, or my organization learn?

14. What did I discover about what needs to be done next?

15. What's not going as well for me in my job now, compared with the way it was before?

16. What's going better for me in my job now, compared with the way it was before?

This chapter is full of useful tools that you can immediately put to use as a coach. Developing goals that are specific, measurable, agreed-upon, realistic, and time-bound will lead to defined actions. The creation of a working action plan allows prioritization, focus, and tracking throughout the coaching process. Assigned supportive activities can ensure step-by-step progress for your clients as they experiment with field practice, role plays, and journaling. Throughout your coaching, you should emphasize ongoing measurement through the creative use of mini-feedback surveys, direct observation checklists, quantitative gap analysis, self-assessment, and action plan self-evaluation. Consequently, the combination of coaching dialogue and supportive tools provides a strong base for discovery, change, and growth.

Moving Ideas to Action

 As a way to combine the many techniques covered in this chapter, practice on yourself! Think of something you would like to master in your coaching toolkit, and complete the application template in table 7-5.

Table 7-5. Personal Action Plan.

1. One of my personal goals for becoming a masterful coach is

2. A SMART objective that will help me achieve this goal is

3. Measurement tools I will use to collect data on my present level of expertise are

4. Tactics and steps I will take are

5. Resources I will use to assist me on this are

6. A mid-course assessment tool I will use to track my progress is

7. Something I will do if I begin to lose focus is

8. I will celebrate my success by

Conducting Coaching Meetings

▶ why it is important that all coaching meetings are well structured

▶ how to conduct productive meetings with your client using the COACH model

▶ to identify your client's barriers and suggest strategies to overcome the barriers

▶ what to do if your client does not make progress toward objectives

Introduction: Juanita's Case

Juanita is the manager of a small call center. She was hired one year ago to improve performance of the busy call center, and given the mandate to decrease turnover rates. In the last year, she has earned the respect of the call center employees and turnover has slightly improved. However, performance indicators (orders taken) have not improved and other department managers say that she has not reached out to them. Juanita is extremely busy on the job and has found that the few comments she has received from other managers have not been helpful. In the data feedback meeting with her coach, Juanita agreed to set up meetings with other department managers, but the first one did not go well. Juanita plans to discuss this with her coach at the next coaching meeting.

David is an internal coach. He was asked by the department manager, Juanita's boss, to be her coach. Juanita readily agreed to the coaching relationship. David conducted a 360-degree feedback survey and has conducted a feedback meeting with Juanita. During that feedback meeting, Juanita set two goals:

1. She would set up individual meetings with the other department managers in the next three months to understand the operation and needs of each department.
2. She would improve the orders taken by call center employees by 10 percent over the next six months.

It is now time for David to conduct Juanita's next coaching meeting, and he wants to discuss her progress toward these goals. Below is how their conversation went.

David: Hi, Juanita. How are you?

Juanita: Great, David. How are you?

David: Good. Juanita, I'm eager to hear how you're progressing on your coaching goals. Are there other items for today's agenda before we talk about those goals?

Juanita: No, I'd like to jump into goals and the action plan.

David: Okay. What action steps from your plan have you taken so far?

Juanita: Well, one of my actions was to set up individual meetings with other department managers to understand their needs. I had my first meeting with Steve from finance. It didn't go very well, and I wanted to talk to you about it before I set up any more meetings.

David: We can definitely discuss that. Anything else?

Juanita: I guess that's it.

David: So, Juanita, is your objective today to talk about the interaction with Steve?

Juanita: Yes, to figure out what went wrong.

David: How would figuring out what went wrong contribute toward your coaching goals of understanding the operation and needs of each department head?

Juanita: Hmmm. By thinking through the effect of what I said and did, I can more readily realize the gap between what actually happened versus what I intended. From there, I can determine alternative approaches. Overall, this would help me determine a different way of communicating that would be more successful in determining the needs of the other department managers.

David: How will you know if a different way can be or is successful?

Juanita: Well, I'll know it is successful if I use the different technique and Steve and other department managers don't get defensive.

David: Great, Juanita! So let's talk about what you did say and what some alternatives might be.

(The dialogue continues with many alternatives discussed.)

David: Well, Juanita, we've discussed many ways you can approach Steve and how you can respond if he gets defensive. What specifically are you going to do?

Juanita: Well, I really like the idea of slowing the pace and asking him more questions. I think I argued with him too much and didn't listen enough. I think I need to let him know that I can appreciate his perspective. I need to stop using words like "should" and phrases like "that won't work." I also want to invite him to visit the call center and listen to some of our calls—I think he would be enlightened!

David: When are you going to meet with Steve next?

Juanita: I'm going to call him tomorrow and set up a meeting for next week.

David: On a scale of one to 10, how committed are you to taking these actions?

Juanita: Put me down for a 10!

Exploring goal opportunities, objectives, and alternative actions is best done within a well-structured coaching meeting. By using an organized approach, you can guide your coaching client, formulate powerful questions, maintain focus, and conclude each meeting with your client committing to taking action. This chapter offers a four-step model that you can use to plan and conduct successful coaching meetings. Since coaching meetings happen throughout a coaching relationship—and progress through various stages—this activity is noted under the process side of the organizational coaching model depicted in figure 8-1.

Figure 8-1. Organizational Coaching Model.

CONTENT

Defining the Role

Collecting and Analyzing Coaching Data

Designing Goals and Tracking Progress

Managing the Coaching Program

PROCESS

Building the Foundation

Co-Creating the Partnership

Feeding Back Coaching Data

Conducting Coaching Meetings

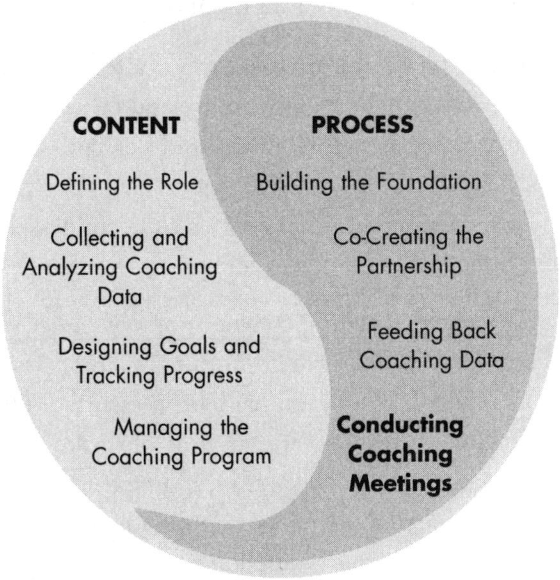

Adapted from *The Organizational Coaching Model*, Bianco-Mathis, Nabors, and Roman (2007).

The COACH Model

The COACH model is a model for conducting an actual coaching meeting. There are four easy phases that provide an excellent framework for a productive coaching meeting:

C   =   Current Situation
O   =   Objectives
A   =   Alternatives
CH =   Choices.

C is for Current Situation. The first phase of conducting a successful coaching meeting is devoted to describing the current situation. This entails getting the clients' feedback on their perceptions of what has transpired since the last coaching meeting. It may include the status of actions committed to on the action plan or new, emergent issues that were unanticipated but ever so common in organizational life. In a sense, this discussion is empowering the client to set the agenda for the coaching meeting. Getting mutual clarity on the current situation is necessary to establish clear, realistic objectives for development.

O is for Objectives. Once the current situation is mutually understood, the coach and client determine the coaching goals, desired results, and measurable objectives (for the particular coaching meeting or for the overall coaching process). Even the most seasoned coaches will tell you how easy it is to slip into friendly conversation that bears no resemblance to coaching when the focus is not on monitoring progress toward objectives.

A is for Alternatives. In this phase, it is time to explore alternative approaches and ideas to reach the desired objectives. Use brainstorming and other techniques to help your clients surface their reasoning, beliefs, feelings, and perceptions. Refrain from offering your ideas, especially at the beginning of this step. Use powerful inquiries to encourage your clients to discover their own resourcefulness in generating ideas. Remember that this is the fertile ground where profound change occurs.

CH is for Choices. A successful coaching conversation concludes with a choice to take action, even if that conscious action is to do nothing. Choices for action may include next steps, milestones, and how success will be measured. The dialogue around choices should also include a realistic appraisal of obstacles and how to overcome them, resources, and support needed. Sometimes, time constraints during the coaching meeting require abbreviated dialogue or completion as a homework assignment. In any case, they are important aspects of choice making and action planning.

Inquiry and Advocacy Within the COACH Model

Let's look back at the coaching dialogue between David and Juanita. You may notice that David inquired about Juanita's current situation with the question, "What action steps from your plan have you taken so far?" That's an excellent question that will give him up-to-date information on Juanita's progress toward her coaching objectives. What if Juanita had said that she had not completed any of her action items because she was too busy? What would have been your reply? This is an excellent opportunity for advocacy, such as "I'm concerned that coaching seems to have a lower priority than everything else. Is that a correct assumption on my part?"

While inquiry and other powerful questions are often the tools of choice for successful coaches, you may find that advocacy is appropriate when following the COACH model during a coaching session. As we discussed in chapter 4, advocacy is a powerful dialogue tool for testing reasoning, fostering inclusion, and offering ideas. Let's look at ways to use both inquiry and advocacy for each step in the COACH model.

Phase 1: Current Situation
Inquiry

- What is the current situation in detail?
- What is the effect of this current situation on you?
- How much control do you have over this situation?
- What action steps have you taken on it so far?

Advocacy

- Here is the current situation as I see it.
- I am concerned about it for the following reasons.
- Let's talk about the control you have over the situation.
- Here are the issues as I see them and why.

While David chose an inquiry to open his coaching dialogue with Juanita, under what circumstances might advocacy have been appropriate? Perhaps if David had been Juanita's supervisor and he was using coaching techniques, he might have chosen to open his coaching meeting with Juanita with the following statement, "Juanita, I am concerned about your relationships with the other department heads. They don't believe you understand their needs and, as I understand it, you have only met with one department head since we last met. Is that correct?"

Phase 2: Objectives

Inquiry

- ▶ What objectives do we need to address at this meeting?
- ▶ How can we make these objectives measurable?
- ▶ Has anything changed with this objective since our last meeting?

Advocacy

- ▶ Here are the objectives we need to address at this meeting.
- ▶ The objectives have changed in the following ways since our last meeting.
- ▶ I'd like to get this far today (at this meeting).

In organizational coaching, the objectives reflect both the needs of the organization as well as the individual or the team being coached. In the case of David and Juanita, it would be appropriate for David to inquire when and how Juanita intended to address the performance improvement goal. He could use advocacy or inquiry depending on what fits the moment or his style. The coach may also use advocacy to interject some realism into the conversation about the meeting's objectives. For example, a coach might say, "It's great that you want to improve all of these team relationships. Let's build some concrete strategies that you can use tomorrow when you will be leading the weekly team meeting. How does that sound?"

Phase 3: Alternatives

Inquiry

- ▶ What are the ways you could approach the issue?
- ▶ What are the advantages and disadvantages of each alternative?
- ▶ Which alternative will have the greatest effect on you? On your organization?
- ▶ Which alternative will get you closest to your goal?

Advocacy

- ▶ You could approach the issue in the following ways.
- ▶ Here are the advantages as I see them and why.
- ▶ Here are the disadvantages as I see them and why.
- ▶ I like the following solution for the following reason.

Your balance of advocacy and inquiry at the alternatives stage in the COACH model will be influenced by a number of factors. Depending on the nature of the topic under discussion, your organizational knowledge may tempt you to offer your own ideas as alternatives. Be careful not to take on the role of consultant here! However, if you are a coaching leader, this is a teachable moment and you can offer ideas for your client to consider in the mix of alternatives. Remember that the ultimate goal is to help your client learn and get results, so let your client make the ultimate choice among the alternatives generated.

Phase 4: Choices

Inquiry

▶ What specifically are you going to do?

▶ When are you going to accomplish this?

▶ What could I do to support you?

▶ On a scale of one to 10, how committed are you to taking these actions?

Advocacy

▶ Here are the decisions I would support and why.

▶ I suggest you should do this by the following deadline.

▶ I will support you by doing the following.

▶ I need to hear your commitment to this plan.

Commitment is very different from conversation and the act of commitment to a choice or to a decision is enhanced by supporting it with a date on the calendar and a number on a scale. Many coaches up the ante of support by offering to send daily emails to their clients to further solidify the commitment to action. David could have ended his dialogue with Juanita by offering to support her (advocacy) in a mutually satisfactory way. The more the coach can reinforce the commitment with links to the documented action plan, quantifiable measures of progress, and motivational tools, the better the chances for coaching success.

The Stuck Client

Coaches have a vision of the perfect client who makes regular progress from coaching meeting to coaching meeting—thanks to our awesome coaching—until graduation day when our client thanks us and happily goes back to the job where all the learning from coaching applies immediately and perfectly. If only that were true!

The reality is that most clients get stuck along the path of coaching for one reason or another. Perhaps crises occur in the job that derail the coaching process. Or perhaps the client tries a strategy; it doesn't work as well as anticipated and the client becomes discouraged. There are many reasons for steady progress to be impeded.

Katie's Case

Katie is director of media strategies for a national volunteer organization. She hired a coach with the approval of the chief executive officer to develop her leadership skills. Her data collection revealed that Katie was admired for her technical skills and that her co-workers felt intimidated by her controlling, non-participative management style. Over the course of her coaching partnership, Katie began to adopt more collaborative, team leadership strategies, and she was encouraged by her team's reaction. Then, a new vice president was hired and became Katie's supervisor. Within a few weeks, it became clear that Katie's new boss was going to be very involved in Katie's work. Katie became angry, fearful, and defensive about her role and her work. Her interest in her coaching objectives changed to, "How can I get my boss off my back?"

One dimension of conducting effective coaching meetings is recognizing when your clients are stuck and helping them to break free. Three common elements that cause clients to become stuck are fear, ego, or impatience (Staub 2002).

Fear is a common barrier, trapping coaching clients in a cycle of inaction, defending intentions, and interpreting or explaining away others' perceptions. A well-thought-out defense allows the clients to protect the ideal self-image that they have created. Most clients are afraid of change, the unknown, and failure. What is your coaching strategy? Name the fear when you hear it. Discuss its benefits and drawbacks. Ask what your clients would choose if they weren't afraid. When you make fear discussable, it tends not to be so scary. In Katie's case, her coach helped Katie to talk about her fear that her boss would derail her career. Once that fear was articulated, a secondary fear emerged—the fear of letting Katie's boss know how her involvement was affecting her and discussing mutual expectations.

Ego is a barrier to change that often is perceived as arrogance. Employees are usually rewarded for a combination of technical and interpersonal skills. Ironically, the same interpersonal behaviors that served them well in a more junior position may now be getting in the way. Getting the work done through others may now be more important than individual contributions. Your job as coach is to help your clients set aside their egos so they hear feedback and use it to grow and develop. Discuss how perceptions by others are critical to success. Help your clients reframe what success looks like. Katie was defensive about her work and not open to her boss's input. Her coach helped her see how that would be perceived by her boss and how that would not help her achieve her career goals.

Both clients and organizational stakeholders may become impatient to see coaching results. Being action-oriented and results-focused is great, and changing behavior and maintaining it takes time and practice. Your strategy to overcome impatience is to address the potential expectation for immediate change right from the beginning and throughout the coaching relationship. Help your client and the entire organization exercise patience, support, and perspective. Hold out for long-term, sustainable change to be the ultimate goal. Katie's coach helped Katie see how patience with her new boss and her own career objectives would help her to be successful in the long term. Her coach encouraged Katie to expand her thinking and to view the situation from her boss's perspective and not just from her own perspective.

As you coach your clients, you may hear a range of expressions that signal they are feeling stuck. Table 8-1 lists some of the more common ones that you might hear with some possible coaching responses. Some responses are useful in more than one kind of stuck scenario.

Table 8-1. Helping Your Clients Get Unstuck.

What You Might Hear	Potential Coaching Responses
1. There are no good options.	• What are the consequences of doing nothing? • Let's lay out all the options. We can pick one that has the most payoff.
2. I tried that. It doesn't work.	• What would work? • How is this situation the same as before? How is it different than in your previous experience?
3. Setting goals is a waste of time. Things change too fast here.	• Are goals helpful to you in general? • How can goals be created that can withstand change?
4. It's not my fault.	• How does blaming others help you?
5. There's no time.	• What can you do in the time you do have? • From past experience, how long does it usually take for a new habit to take hold?
6. This goal won't be rewarded here.	• What can you do to change things? • How do you know that this goal isn't rewarded here? What is rewarded here? • What motivates you other than outside rewards?
7. I don't want to hurt his feelings.	• How likely is that to happen? How do you know? • What are the consequences of not giving him this information/feedback? • How does not giving him this information/feedback help him?
8. I don't want to rock the boat.	• What would happen if you rocked the boat? • How is this rocking the boat? • What are the consequences of doing nothing?
9. You don't understand how things work around here.	• That may be true. What does it take to be effective here? • How might you take this and modify it to fit how things are done around here?

This chapter emphasizes the necessity of planning each coaching meeting and using a systematic approach. Winging it is not acceptable. The dialogue within each meeting should follow the same four-step process: define the current situation, establish the working objective, explore alternatives, and choose specific actions. By following such a process, you can smoothly conclude every meeting with direct actions to be practiced before the next meeting. Such a system establishes purpose and flow. The four-step process provides a mental checklist for the coach and a structured framework for the client. With such a roadmap, you will be able to concentrate and address barriers that often creep into the coaching process—fear, ego, and impatience. You can break cycles of inaction and defensiveness and provide the necessary perspective to guide the client toward new behaviors.

Moving Ideas to Action

You can use the following application to practice using the COACH model in a situation that is relevant for your workplace. Ask someone from your workplace to practice with you. First, think of a pertinent coaching situation within your workplace and discuss the following elements:

1. What is the role of the coaching client?
2. What is the role of the coach (internal, external, etc.)?
3. What is the coaching objective?
4. What is the status of the coaching relationship (new, data feedback meeting, well-established coaching relationship, etc.)?
5. What is the goal of the coaching meeting?

After discussing the coaching situation, determine who will be the coach and who will be the client. The coach should use a balance of inquiry and advocacy and use the COACH model as an aid. After the practice, discuss the following questions:

1. How did the coach ascertain the
   - current situation
   - objectives
   - alternatives
   - choices?
2. How did the client respond?
3. What challenges did the coach experience? How were they handled?
4. What alternative behaviors might you suggest?

Managing the Coaching Program

······· **In this chapter, you'll learn** ·······

▶ the first steps to starting an organizational coaching program

▶ techniques for selling and negotiating a coaching program to achieve organizational buy-in

▶ the next steps in building an entire coaching infrastructure

▶ how to measure return-on-investment at many levels

▶ how to navigate inevitable challenges

Introduction: Coaching Task Force Case

Below is part of the proceedings from the second meeting of the Coaching Task Force (CTF) for HiTec, a large technology company. The meeting is being facilitated by the vice president of human resources, Mark Ryan. Participants include members of the human resources staff and representatives from various divisions, locations, and levels throughout the company. During the first meeting, everyone agreed on the need and value of implementing a coaching program and developed a list of action items, concerns, and general goals.

> **Mark:** I'm really excited about you all agreeing to be part of the CTF, and I think we all agree that we have a lot of work ahead of us. We all seem to be aligned on the need and value of introducing a coaching program within HiTec. As a reminder, our objective today is to brainstorm the characteristics and components of the kind of program we would like at HiTec. We will then consolidate all of our thoughts into a formal project plan and submit it to the Executive Board for review and acceptance. As I explained last time, the board has blessed the idea in theory, and now a complete business plan is required. So, as we brainstorm today, I'll jot down our ideas on the flipcharts.

Jan, marketing director: Mark, I shared our preliminary thoughts from the first meeting with my department, and they have a few suggestions. Specifically, they have a concern about confidentiality and how the coaching program will tie to performance appraisals and other developmental activities already provided by the company.

Mark: Excellent points. Let's continue the list we started last time. Obviously, we need to develop very clear confidentiality guidelines. Also, we need to be very clear on how coaching is going to be aligned with our other programs.

Bob, director from Dallas: Yes, that's my concern. For example, let's say I already have a mentor, do I also get a coach? And if I do, what's the difference?

Mark: Exactly. We want to make sure we demonstrate how coaching is part of our total systems approach and how an employee may choose certain avenues of development in combination or separately with other tools. For example, a person might take part in a 360-degree evaluation, choose to have a coach to assist in developmental areas, sign up for attendance at our six-month leadership development program, and work with a mentor who might help with advice on how to get into sales or international work. Folks need to experience the elements of the system in a distinct yet mutually beneficial way.

Angela, member of the training department: I like the linking idea and think those of us in HR need to be particularly sensitive to making sure those linkages happen. I have another concern, however, and it has to do with money. Let's face it, this is going to require resources, and I want to be the first to put my personal agenda right on the table. How is this program going to affect the limited resources we have? I'm concerned that money that might otherwise go to training or one of our other successful programs might now go to the coaching program instead. I think we have to be careful about hurting the programs we already have.

Mark: I understand your concern, Angela, and I support the notion of maintaining the integrity of our existing programs. We need to consider the financial resources and allocations in our cost-benefit analysis. Because of this, we might need to present a staged approach as opposed to offering coaching to everyone at once. Given systems thinking, we might treat our developmental activities like our flexible benefit accounts where each person is allocated a certain amount of dollars for development and he or she then has choices among our various developmental options. That's just an idea, but we need to be creative.

Dina, director from New York: That's a good idea, Mark. Building off of that, I think we need to learn from our experience with introducing our benefits plan three years ago. We did not do a very good job of educating everyone, and there were delayed services and a lot of confusion. I suggest we create a comprehensive communications plan, complete with focus groups, articles in the newsletter, and department visits. There are going to be many people who don't know what coaching is and others who might have the wrong idea. So, we almost need a marketing campaign around this.

Latasha, member of the information technology department: Being the voice of technology, we need to identify the technology needs and parameters.

Eric, vice president of finance: And knowing Linda [the president of the company], I think we all know we have to be very clear on how the coaching program supports our strategic goals. The project plan should include a strong business case, explaining how a coaching program meets our bottom-line needs and the consequences of not having one.

Mark: I'll put that down at the top of the list, Eric.

Larry, member of the human resources employee relations: A good thing here is that we developed and published such great HR guidelines last year. Now all we would need to do is add a chapter on coaching, so that should work out well. I would like us to describe the entire process, complete with examples and directions for participation. I don't want anyone to be able to say that they weren't informed—which brings us to the importance of educating all managers so they can appropriately guide and support the program.

Mark: Great, Larry, we don't want managers falling through the cracks. Something we also have to work through is whether we are going to use internal coaches, external coaches, or some kind of combination. We need to create clear parameters on a typical coaching engagement and provide tools for tracking and measuring all aspects of the program. That goes back to what you said, Eric. We need continual data to keep the program energized, supported, effective, and efficient.

Well, it seems like the CTF is off to a good start! Members of the team are raising important issues that will need to be researched, planned, sorted, negotiated, and tested. The considerations are multidimensional. The entire program needs to support the organization's strategic plan while also meeting the individual developmental needs of employees. There are cost implications and personal agendas concerning areas of accountability, resources, and various stakeholders. Employees need to be educated, and managers must buy in to the process. Careful communication is necessary so coaching is viewed as a benefit for growth, not as a punishment for poor performance. Proper protocol must be followed in presenting a business plan, justifying the resources, and outlining the benefits. Details and guidelines must be understood, measured, and fairly used.

The workplace learning and performance coach can be the best coach in the world, and yet be thwarted by inconsistent practices, budget constraints, or lack of stakeholder buy-in. Conflicting agendas, conflicts with other learning or human resources programs within the organization, poor communication, and ignorance of the program benefits and goals can undermine success. Planning a coaching program for your organization is a challenging task. Such planning requires creativity and attention to details. An important point to remember during planning is that the process is iterative. You and others will move forward and backward and will cycle through steps several times as pieces of the plan take shape.

This culminating chapter steps up to embrace the bigger picture: planning and managing of the coaching program. We will discuss the elements of designing, implementing, and managing a coaching program at the individual, team, and organizational levels: apply a systems approach, create a program vision, assess an organization's readiness, develop a set of guidelines and steps, sell the program and negotiate roles, measure and publicize results, and navigate common challenges. As

Figure 9-1. Organizational Coaching Model.

Adapted from *The Organizational Coaching Model*, Bianco-Mathis, Nabors, and Roman (2007).

demonstrated in the case study, planning is necessary before coaching is actually initiated within an organization. However, we discuss planning and managing last as a way to bring all the pieces together. This step is posted on the content side of the overall organizational coaching model in figure 9-1 because details around vision, guidelines, roles, and measures must be included within a coaching infrastructure.

Throughout this chapter, we will follow Mark and the CTF team as they tackle each planning and management component.

Apply a Systems Approach

This chapter comes full circle as we re-emphasize the necessity of using a systems approach to integrate a coaching program with all stakeholders, organizational roles, and learning programs within an organization, as shown in figure 9-2. It is important to link any coaching program with existing infrastructures, such as performance appraisals, 360-degree inventories, career development tools, needs assessment surveys, organizational surveys, leadership competency models, training programs, and other developmental tools. When an integrated approach is used, a coaching program can further reinforce and build an entire learning organization and support organizational drivers.

Figure 9-2. Systems Coaching Approach.

All systems within an organization influence one another. Adding or modifying one system affects all other systems. By factoring this synergistic effect within the design and implementation of a coaching program, maximum benefit to the organization can be achieved.

There are two major levels of coordination that require attention when facilitating a systems coaching approach. One level is the interactions and agreements that need to be made among stakeholders of related programs. As pointed out in the initial scenario, managers of various functions need to be part of the process so roles can be clarified. If coordination of the training, mentoring, and career development programs within a company sits within different roles, then these professionals need to meet on a regular basis to streamline processes and work through any emerging conflicts— among themselves and among their programs. They need to make sure consistent messages begin in recruitment, move through training programs, are reinforced through performance appraisals, and are supported by mentors. For example, if the director of training is working against the director of career development and coaching, there might be resource imbalances, perpetuation of programs based on power instead of need, or open conflict at meetings and in departmental goal setting.

The second level of systems attention involves the employees. Employees and managers should be educated in how to build development plans that integrate the various tools that the organization offers. This plan needs to be orchestrated so an employee's involvement is focused on designated goals. Participation cannot be random. Consequently, an employee might work out a plan with a manager that includes attending an outside training course in presentation skills, working with a coach for six sessions on stage presence, and attending a session at the career center on transfer possibilities into public relations.

A coaching program is meant to be linked to other enrichment processes within the organization. If an employee is working with a coach and also participates in the mentorship program and the 360-degree assessment process, the coach should help the employee coordinate the actions and outputs of all three processes. A systems approach leads to integrated results. A non-systems approach leads to disjointed results.

Create a Vision

Futurist Joel Barker says, "Vision without action is a dream. Action without vision is merely passing time. Vision and action can change the world" (*The Power of Vision* 1993). Before embarking on the implementation of a coaching program, it is necessary to brainstorm the overall purpose and objectives of the system you are creating. First, you need to answer the question, "What organizational drivers are pointing to the need and purpose of a coaching program?" You need to paint a picture of how the program will look; what it will achieve; what the outcomes will be; and what the benefits will be for individuals, teams, and the organization. Just as organizations create visions—a future picture of what they are striving for—a coaching program should also embody a vision. You can begin to develop such a vision by considering the following questions:

- ▶ Why should we have a coaching program?
- ▶ What will the benefits of a coaching program be?
- ▶ What organizational drivers will be fulfilled through such a program?
- ▶ What else within the organization would support such a program?
- ▶ How would such a program support our culture and organizational goals and values?
- ▶ What would be the outcomes of such a program (for individuals, teams, and the organization)?

As the vice president of finance expressed within the CTF, it is important to be able to explain how coaching supports organizational strategies and goals. What will a coaching program do? For example, might it

- ▶ create more competent executives who can build stronger teams
- ▶ align personal goals with organizational goals and reduce turnover
- ▶ create aligned structures and processes for increased productivity

- ▶ establish a culture of learning, dialogue, and continuous improvement so higher goals and results become more of a norm
- ▶ create a high-performance organization and better meet bottom-line success?

An example of the organizational drivers and vision that the CTF developed for HiTec is in exhibit 9-1. The format is less important than presenting an energizing future picture that drives people to action.

Assess Organizational Readiness

Even a clear, well-developed vision will not guarantee success in a nonsupportive climate. Questions to consider when analyzing the readiness of an organization are outlined in exhibit 9-2. A negative answer to any of the questions does not mean you can't implement a coaching program; rather, it merely indicates that you need to plan around the challenge and put contingency efforts in place.

Exhibit 9-1. Organizational Drivers and Vision.

The following business needs are strengthened through the coaching program at HiTec:

- constant focus on customer service so service becomes our signature reputation
- mutual support in performance management so there is continuous improvement within every job and our human resources are challenged and used effectively
- open dialogue and efficient project management to facilitate good decisions, quality outputs, and productive teams
- strategic thinking so we maintain a future-focused organization, emphasizing leading-edge thoughts, ideas, and goals
- increased commitment toward goal fulfillment and alignment of personal goals with organizational goals
- alignment of all systems within the organization so our infrastructure supports what we do and what we say.

The benefits and overall vision of having our coaching program include

- providing one-on-one development assistance to those who wish to engage in a coaching relationship
- fostering continuous improvement for individuals, teams, and the organization
- supporting a culture of continuous learning
- legitimizing the coaching process as an active developmental tool that is acceptable and as comfortable as training, seminars, team building, or online resources
- creating the process of coaching as a common performance improvement tool
- implementing coaching dialogue as the main communication language
- creating a high-performance organization
- supporting the implementation of individual, group, and organizational goals and strategies.

Exhibit 9-2. Assess Organizational Readiness.

1. Does the organization believe in continuous learning and change, or is the status quo valued above all else?

2. Is there a history or precedent within the organization for allocating money toward development programs? Is it valued? Is it considered during the budgeting process?

3. Is there internal or external staff available to be coaches? Will the organization dedicate the time and money for developing coaches and allowing employees to participate in coaching sessions?

4. Does the culture support openness, confrontation, honesty, and dialogue—or is it best to hide information?

5. Is it safe for employees to tell the truth and say what they feel without fear of confidences being broken or being punished for honesty?

6. Is information freely shared, or is communication stifled?

7. Are there other learning structures in the organization that the coaching program can depend on, be linked with, or build on?

8. Is the human resources department valued and credible, or is it seen as merely a compliance department?

9. Are managers encouraged or measured on how well they develop their employees?

10. Are employees encouraged to grow and develop?

11. Would the organization more readily accept internal coaches or external coaches or a combination?

12. Are there a place and personnel available to manage the program?

13. How have other programs been successfully implemented within the organization?

For example, if your organization is skeptical about the benefits of coaching, you can suggest a pilot program and then widely communicate the bottom-line results with top decision makers. Having a highly regarded executive take part in the pilot and then singing its praises can greatly influence implementation. This kind of buy-in also demonstrates a positive image of coaching and the perpetuation of a culture that values feedback and growth. For this reason, it is common for organizations to initiate coaching with the top executive group and to tie coaching to identified leadership competencies.

Design the Program

Once you have developed a vision and assessed the organization's readiness, it is time to create the overall design of the program. This is the guts of the planning: What will the program look like and how will it be run? A design has many components that must be integrated into a coordinated whole. Each component must be researched, thought through, and outlined in appropriate detail to be carried out. Since a plan must be tailored to a specific organization, it takes time and cannot be completed overnight. The checklist in exhibit 9-3 can guide you through a design process.

Coaches need to consider all facets of the program—from budget, roles, administration, tools, and policies to identifying specific coaches, formatting typical coaching situations, matching coaches with clients, communicating results, and working with stakeholders.

Exhibit 9-3. Coaching Program Design Checklist.

- Establish whether external coaches, internal coaches, or a combination will be used.
- Develop criteria and processes for choosing, educating, orientating, tracking, and measuring coaches and allocating time.
- Investigate and determine costs and how costs will be budgeted and tracked.
  — If internal, where will the costs be allocated?
  — If external, what will the cost and payment structure be?
- Establish guidelines for who can be coached, by whom, and the process for matching coaches and clients.
- Define the levels or job categories to be coached.
- Decide which types of coaching are appropriate and in which situations.
- Determine who will own and be administratively responsible for running the program.
- Establish how the program will be communicated: online, brochures, written guidelines, policy manual.
- Establish roles and protocol among key stakeholders: coach, client, client's manager, human resource, leadership, owners of other related programs.
- Determine the kind of data gathering that is appropriate—surveys, 360-degree instruments, paper and pencil, online, internally developed, off-the-shelf, style or personality inventory—as well as costs involved, how data will be shared, and with whom.
- Outline what a typical meeting or coaching engagement might include and look like, and create guidelines and formats to be followed.
- Determine typical coaching challenges, and include guidelines for how to handle such challenges: confidentiality break, coach and client not getting along, manager wanting coach to perform management duties, client needing therapy instead of coaching.
- Develop guidelines for how coaches, clients, and the program will be measured, and determine the necessary infrastructure to support such measurement.
- Determine what is necessary to sell and market the program to all constituents and how that will be done.
- Decide what other programs or infrastructures may be necessary to support a successful coaching program: 360-degree instruments, established competencies for leadership development, career opportunities, the concept of coaching embedded in training programs, the concept of dialogue embedded in coaching programs, technology support, organizational surveys, goal-oriented performance appraisals, clear role descriptions and expectations, information-sharing culture.
- Who has access to what information, and under what circumstances?

The planning results for HiTec and the decisions the CTF made to support the program's vision are displayed in exhibit 9-4. Although you are encouraged to create a design based on the specific needs of your organization, this design is a typical one.

Sell the Program and Negotiate Roles

When trying to convince an organization to introduce a coaching program, it is important to educate while gaining support. People will want to know how this program relates to other programs, how the program benefits them and the organization, the process and guidelines for participating, the budget and costs, and the overall roles and expectations. You need to implement a carefully crafted negotiation strategy where you stipulate the key stakeholders, think through conflicting

---

Exhibit 9-4. HiTec Coaching Program Design.

- Coaching guidelines are available on the company intranet and are reviewed and updated every year. The guidelines provide administrative procedures and also define coaching, outline the typical process, and provide research and additional resources concerning the field of coaching.

- The coaching program is administered through a CTF with special decisions escalated to the Executive Committee. The vice president of human resources sits on the CTF to provide assistance with issues requiring human resource expertise and coordination.

- A pool of external coaches (who meet our contract requirements concerning expertise and experience) are available for director-level positions and above.

- Internal coaches—specially trained in the coaching discipline and who meet established criteria in terms of training and certification—are available for employees below the director level.

- Costs of the program are embedded in each department's training and development budget. There is also a corporate coaching budget managed through human resources to support administrative activities, ongoing development of internal coaches, and special cases where additional funds might be necessary.

- Employees and their managers discuss and decide whether coaching should be a part of a particular person's development plan, along with other developmental activities, such as career development, training, mentoring, and job rotation.

- Based on specified needs and goals of the coaching, each person is given three possible coaches to interview and then a formal match is made.

- The formal coaching process includes six one-hour meetings, usually a combination of telephone and in-person meetings. Coach and client stipulate the exact schedule and develop a coaching agreement.

- The coaching process will include the gathering of data from at least two sources: 360-degree instruments, one-on-one interviews, open-ended surveys, personal inventories.

- The coaching between a coach and client is confidential. The only information a coach might be required to report are
  — the dates of all coaching meetings conducted
  — a start-up coaching list that the coach completes with the client at the beginning of the process
  — a completed coaching checklist that the coach completes with the client at the end of the process.

---

agendas, and navigate the political climate within the organization. You must use your best dialogue techniques to create win-win situations. Components to include in your marketing strategy are listed in exhibit 9-5.

Exhibit 9-5. Selling the Program.

1. Consider key stakeholders, link your agenda to their agenda, and strategize appropriate negotiation strategies for ownership.

2. Relate the coaching program to all other pertinent programs, and demonstrate mutual support.

3. Carefully plan costs, both short-term and long-term, and develop a cost-benefit analysis.

4. Prepare support materials, charts, graphs, role descriptions, and other marketing materials to guide your implementation plan.

5. Assess political climate within the organizational culture, and plan for contingencies, formal and informal power channels, decision makers, and how things usually get done throughout the organization.

6. Develop dialogue meetings and presentations, and obtain the assistance of key supporters to move the implementation forward.

7. Network and get in front of allies, advocates, and stakeholders.

Selling a coaching program to key stakeholders within an organization is similar to any other business proposal that decision makers face. Holding problem-solving discussions and working through possible glitches up front lessen the chances of future conflicts. An ideal strategy is to conduct a series of information sessions with management and employee groups to pave the way, gain support, and foster excitement. Special attention needs to be paid to three groups: decision makers, stakeholders who might have conflicting agendas, and managers.

Decision makers need to be part of the planning process at the very beginning. Presenting a cogent business plan that outlines costs and benefits is essential to gaining organizational support.

Holding small-group or one-on-one meetings with key stakeholders is essential in stipulating boundaries, ensuring that each person's agenda is being considered, and building a partnership with those who might otherwise derail your efforts. People are more inclined to support an activity if their input has been solicited, valued, and incorporated into the process.

Lastly, managers need to be engaged. Management ranks within organizations can make or break a program. It is important to provide managers clear, step-by-step guidelines, scenarios of coaching working and not working, and tools that can be used to facilitate the process. Managers are pulled in many directions. They will more readily use and support a program that is user-friendly and accompanied by an actual roadmap.

Measure Process and Results

Once the coaching program is in motion, the job has just begun. Like any well-run machine, the program needs to be continually monitored, tracked, and maintained. It is important to demonstrate return-on-investment at many levels. This requires clear responsibility, measurement tools, continuous improvement of policies and procedures, and ongoing communication with the entire organization.

The various measurement categories that should be tracked within a coaching program are outlined in table 9-1. Tools and actions for each category are listed. Many of these tools are purposefully repetitive, and it is wise to create tools that evaluate more than one dimension at a time. For example, a well-worded survey can measure the success of a team that has been coached, the actual outcomes demonstrated, the coach involved, and the budget and costs that were spent.

Dedicating resources to measurement tracking and analysis needs to be incorporated into the coaching program in the planning stages. Otherwise, like so many other organizational activities, the effect of the work is never acknowledged nor realized. Data are needed to make ongoing decisions concerning the viability of the program and to make adjustments and modifications to meet the changing needs of the organization. If the strategic goals of a company change, leadership competencies shift, financial resources decline, or the organizational structure is realigned, the effect of these trends need to be incorporated into the coaching process.

In addressing the measurement of executive coaching, Phillips and Phillips (2005) reminds practitioners to evaluate levels of satisfaction, learning, on-the-job application, business effect, and return-on-investment. Gathering such coaching measures can be part of a larger measurement activity or a solo effort. For example, a survey might be distributed to those who have been coached and questions might center only on the coaching experience. Or a longer employee climate survey might be used that asks a series of questions on several human resource activities: coaching, performance management, training, mentoring.

Coaches should create a tool that incorporates Phillips and Phillips's five areas of measurement. Results can then be efficiently communicated and managed in the following four categories.

Table 9-1. Measurement Categories and Ideas.

What to Measure	How to Measure
Track budgets and costs.	• Accounting categories established for coaching costs and listed as separate line items • Coaching spreadsheets or reports designated to track coaching costs and incorporated into the budgeting process and reviews • Coaching costs designated as either centralized or part of department budgets • Cost-benefit analyses for yearly coaching report (relating coaching to positive outcomes within the organization)
Evaluate effectiveness of the administration and process.	• Surveys of managers using coaching for their staff • Focus groups and interviews with those involved in coaching • Audit and process improvement sessions with those managing or administrating the process • Roundtable discussion
Evaluate external and internal coaches.	• Formatted status reports on a scheduled basis • Status meetings on a scheduled basis • Surveys of clients with whom the coach interacts • Agreed-upon results within stipulated timeframes and checkpoints (as evaluated through client progress)
Evaluate client progress: Individual.	• Pre- and post-360-degree surveys • Pre- and post-interviews • Periodic behavior surveys • Observation checklists • Action plan tracking • Performance output appraisals • Self-assessments
Evaluate client progress: Team.	• Pre- and post-surveys completed by those who interact with the team • Pre- and post-team member surveys • Facilitator observations • Tracking of team results • Self-assessments
Evaluate client progress: Organization.	• Pre- and post-climate surveys • Pre- and post-customer surveys • Strategic planning progress • Goal achievements • Turnover and recruitment success rates • Success rates of internal systems, procedures, and support structures (evaluated through process-improvement strategies) • Yearly cost-benefit analyses • Number of grievances

Efficiency of the program costs. Work with your accounting department to allocate specific codes that will capture pertinent coaching costs. Possible cost areas might include money spent on outside coaches, partial or total salaries of inside coaches dedicated to coaching, training workshops for internal coaches, coaching guidelines and materials, and data-gathering instruments. It is also useful to capture intangible costs, such as time spent in coaching meetings. In addition, it is also important to note direct and indirect costs due to inefficiencies when coaching is not offered, which should then be aligned with the findings in the fourth area, effectiveness of coaching. For example, time and money lost to conflicts, poor performance, ineffective decisions and interactions, and turnover.

Effectiveness of the administration and process. Areas to explore in administration and process include effectiveness in matching coaches with clients, timeliness and responsiveness of service, clarity and usefulness of the guidelines, number of failed and successful coaching assignments, overall ratings of the pool of external and internal coaches, frequency of use, comparison in relationship to other human resource development programs, and user's assessment of the overall quality.

Competency and effectiveness of coaches. In assessing coaches, it is important to have a preset list of competencies and criteria to measure and rate each coach. Such a list would include many of the characteristics that are outlined in chapter 2: has credentials in coaching methods, follows ethical protocols, establishes ground rules and agreements, stipulates clear goals, upholds confidentiality, treats clients and the organization with respect, develops working action plans, follows the company's administrative procedures in terms of paperwork and accounting, and measures progress.

Effectiveness of the coaching. Two dimensions of coaching need to be measured. The first is a basic comparison of the achievement of goals from the beginning to the end of the coaching assignment: *Were objectives achieved? To what extent have established goals been met? Is there a tangible difference in behaviors or results due to the coaching?* The second dimension is the larger context: *What effect is coaching having on the organization? To what degree has coaching had a positive effect on the overall culture, leadership, and direction of the organization? Through the use of a cost-benefit analysis, how do the monetary benefits of the program compare to the program costs?* In essence, this measure provides the return-on-investment of coaching.

Given that coaching is one of many activities that might influence organizational outcomes, it is helpful to demonstrate the indirect influence of coaching and its role as a key component in overall effectiveness. For example, the cause of decreased turnover in a particular department could be the result of:

- ▶ a new leader positioned in the group
- ▶ a coach working with the new leader

> a coach working with the management team (as a group) within the department
> new technology that streamlines the work processes
> new office space and furniture for that department.

The important message to get across is that coaching is being tracked and included as part of an entire performance effort so its role in success is acknowledged. With the help of trained researchers, more specific and direct measures can be designed and used. Diane Stober, in "Approaches to Research on Executive and Organizational Coaching Outcomes" (2005), cites the results of several research studies on coaching. One study tested the post-coaching behavioral outcomes within *Fortune* 100 companies. The researchers interviewed 75 executives and their coaches. Substantial gains were noted in the areas of:

> task accomplishment (increased effectiveness in staff assignments, staff development, conducting meetings)
> long-term adaptability (increased flexibility, wider repertoire of behavior, increased observation before action)
> personal effectiveness (increased patience, confidence in dealing with superiors)
> identity shifts (increased self-knowledge, self-confidence, validation of views).

A second study tested 100 executives who had been coached. The results of this study demonstrated success in goal achievement, overall satisfaction of both the client and the client's manager, and both tangible and intangible outcomes:

> Eighty-six percent of participants and 74 percent of stakeholders (immediate supervisors and human resource personnel) reported being very satisfied or extremely satisfied with the coaching they or the executive client received.
> Seventy-three percent of established goals were effectively achieved.
> Tangible outcomes included increased productivity, quality, organizational strength, and customer service.
> Intangible outcomes included improved relationships with direct reports, peers, and stakeholders; improved teamwork; increased job satisfaction; and reduced conflict.

The justification for a coaching program is quite simple. When organizations are quick to list required competencies, administer 360-degree evaluations, and allocate goals against which employees are measured, an organization has the obligation to provide tools, avenues, and assistance in achieving what is being demanded. Coaching is an integral part of fulfilling that need.

Publicize Results

It is important to communicate the results of your coaching program so its value can be readily acknowledged. You can create a self-fulfilling cycle where successful coaching leads to successful results, which can easily be done through appropriate communication and the publicizing of results. The list below outlines some ideas for publicizing results and keeping the concept of coaching in the forefront of the organization's agenda:

▶ Publish a monthly coaching tidbits newsletter or segment as part of the organization's newsletter (online or print).

▶ Visit staff meetings around the company, conducting mini-coaching updates, distributing job aids, and increasing learning.

▶ Establish learning community meetings or online interchanges.

▶ Conduct group coaching and team building, using coaching techniques.

▶ Build coaching into existing program protocol (for example, 360-degree surveys every two years for leadership, followed by three coaching meetings).

▶ Have key leaders share their successful coaching experiences at pertinent meetings, training sessions, and other employee gatherings.

▶ Train all managers to be coaches to build an entire coaching culture.

Develop Coaches

For a coaching program to remain strong, participating coaches—whether internal or external—need to keep their skills sharp. As a workplace learning and performance coach, you are a role model for the rest of the organization and you need to present yourself continually in top form. This requires discipline toward skill practice—keeping up with coaching literature and tools, attending workshops, and perhaps pursuing certification through the International Coach Federation. Managing a coaching program must include a development component for all coaches, which can be satisfied through a variety of structures, such as the following:

▶ separate library (room or online resource) for coaching materials

▶ networking opportunities, both internally and externally (This can be formal, such as membership in coaching associations, or informal, such as having lunch with fellow coaches every month.)

▶ monthly coaching forums where coaches meet, discuss successes and challenges, share learning and resources, and perhaps listen to a guest speaker or instructor

▶ yearly seminars on advanced techniques and strategies (internally or externally).

Navigate Challenges

You planned carefully. You have buy-in and support from the organization. Your coaches are off and running, and clients are anxious to be coached. Then, problems begin to surface. Don't panic! This is to be expected. Like any program where people and organizational policies are involved, there will be issues, from interpersonal conflicts to budget cuts. The key is to expect these challenges, plan for them, and move quickly to resolve them. Typical challenges and ideas for managing such situations are discussed below.

The client and coach don't get along. Have guidelines for matching coaches and clients and for making changes when necessary. Your coaching guidelines should clearly outline how coaches are matched with clients (clients should be able to interview two or more coaches and choose) and also give specific steps to be taken if either the coach or the client believes that the match is not working. Causes of a failed match might be many:

- Personality conflicts between coaches and clients.
- The coach does not have the specific expertise that the client needs.
- Clients, for whatever reasons, decide that coaching is not something they want to continue (time involved, discomfort with one-on-one nature).
- A perceived or real issue of trust, confidentiality, or boundaries emerges.
- The coach's style (too passive, too aggressive) does not meet the needs of the client.
- Client keeps canceling and fails to follow agreed-upon ground rules.

A good coach will be able to test whether the problem is one of normal push-back that happens when people have to take accountability for their development versus an underlying problem that is best dealt with by assigning another coach. The organization should also provide the option of having a third-party assess the situation and smoothly negotiate sides. Whatever the reason, feelings must be respected on all sides. This should be done without judgment or blame and simply accepted as something that happens from time to time.

The client blames the coach. Sometimes the coach can become the scapegoat for the client's problems or lack of results. It is important to have regular status meetings and protocols for assessing client involvement and responsibility.

The coach is ineffective. The coach may not be adequately prepared to deal with coaching situations within your organization. Have specific guidelines and checks for coaching competencies and education and specific tools for coach evaluations.

The coach gives advice that is not in line with the corporation. Have coach preparation meetings with coaches, making sure they understand the strategy, culture, climate, processes, and goals of the organization. A coach needs to know enough about the organization to assist the client within the structure and culture of that particular organization. If clients are feeling unfilled because the organization "won't let us do anything," the coach needs to be able to assist the clients in determining how their styles coincide with the organization and the implications of what that may mean.

The client doesn't need coaching. Assess early in the process whether coaching is the best solution for the manifested issues. Be ready to recommend other programs—separately or in combination with the coaching—as appropriate (therapy, employee assistance programs, training, university degree program, on-the-job skill development, outsourcing, career development, process improvement).

External coaches are selling themselves. Make agreements or contracts with all external coaches on what is acceptable and not acceptable in terms of recommending their services to clients within the organization. Usually, when a coach is working with a manager or leader, it is best not to also conduct other organization development work with other members of that same department. It opens the door for issues concerning confidentiality, trust, and conflicting motives.

Administration of the program is poor. Designate a key owner and administrator to coordinate activities, negotiate with other stakeholders throughout the organization, track measures, make decisions, manage resources, and screen coaches. Employees and managers need a designated person to contact concerning questions, process, budget, or special cases.

Coaching surfaces other organizational issues. During the coaching process, an issue might emerge that transcends the client's control. Clarify with clients what is a coaching issue and what might really be a bigger problem in terms of the organizational structure, leadership, job responsibilities, or business processes. It is the coach's job to work with the client in terms of what can be done or not done in working the bigger issue and concentrate on what the client can control. It might also be helpful to have quarterly discussions with all coaches and other human resources or organization development professionals to share organizational trends that seem to be surfacing during performance reviews, coaching sessions, surveys, and other feedback vehicles. It is important to stress that the point of discussion is to identify trends that emerge from composite feedback and interactions, not anything personal or confidential to a particular person or situation.

Through such feedback loops, coaching becomes a part of the organization development strategy. By pooling and focusing on such trends, workplace learning and performance professionals can take positive action toward continuous improvement. For example, if 15 participants in the latest leadership training class and 10 managers involved in coaching all surfaced a problem with the new online budgeting process, that's feedback that should be collated and shared with the appropriate people.

This chapter—the last step of the coaching model—provides the infrastructure for all other steps. Planning must start before a coaching program is ever launched. Managing, measuring, and communicating results of the program must happen throughout the process. When initiating coaching systems within your organizations, coaches should design a process that aligns with other practices, supports strategic goals, fits the culture, and meets the needs of individual employees. Administrators of the program need to be clearly identified, and it is their job to gain buy-in from all stakeholders, work through conflicting agendas, gain financial support, and publish clear guidelines for an efficient and confidential approach. The job aids in this chapter provide an excellent roadmap for the development and implementation of an ethical and successful coaching process.

Moving Ideas to Action

You are a workplace learning and performance professional, and you want to start a coaching program in your organization. Or perhaps there already is a coaching program, and it needs to grow and improve.

If your organization already has a coaching program, use table 9-2 to evaluate the existing program and make recommendations for improvement. If the organization doesn't have a program, use it to design a program that fits your organization. Refer to the charts and checklists throughout this chapter for help in formulating your plan.

Table 9-2. My Coaching Plan Template.

1. Goals/objectives/visions of the program:

2. Other programs within the organization that the coaching program should be linked with:

3. Challenges/readiness issues that need to be handled:

4. Design:
   - Owner/administrator of the program:
   - Type of coaches:
   - Protocols for getting a coach:
   - Typical coaching engagement:
   - Training and qualifications of coaches:
   - Confidentiality issues:
   - Measurement and publicity of results:

5. Strategies for selling the program:

Epilogue

Coaching in general and business coaching in particular have evolved greatly since the late 1980s. At that time, business coaching services were primarily focused on performance and served to close a gap. In the 1990s, practitioners became more mainstream, and businesses began to use coaching as an effective learning and development resource. Coaches are now able to provide one-on-one, just-in-time help to managers, executives, and teams. Their support is customized and targeted. The delivery system is flexible—a combination of in-person, telephone, and email contact is common. The focus is holistic, taking into account a broad view of clients, who they are and how they function within the context of their organizations. Coaching, done well, delivers results, and for organizations, coaching has gained credibility as a viable way to impact the bottom line.

Early on, the relationship between organizations and coaches was ill-defined. Thousands of dollars were spent with hit-or-miss outcomes and unclear ties between the "coaching process" and results. During the past decade, we have seen a shift toward more structure and discipline, a clear coaching process, explicit agreements, targeted goals and outcomes, and follow up.

Many organizations now have created and integrated strong coaching programs and consider coaching to be a key factor in the success of their high-performing managers, executives, and teams. Coaches are working in partnership with clients to facilitate outcomes that transcend traditional training and career development. Organizations who are hoping to raise the bar and create high-performance learning cultures are making coaching a part of the way they do business. It is our intention that the information, charts, examples, and cases provided in this book will help any professional who is interested in doing the same.

References

Argyris, C. *Overcoming Organizational Defenses*. New York: Prentice-Hall, 1990.

Auerbach, J. "Cognitive Coaching." In *Evidence Based Coaching Handbook*, D. Stober and A. Grant, editors. Hoboken, New Jersey: Wiley & Sons, 2006.

Banks, A. "Baby Boomers Can Become a Coach and Mentor." *American Chronicle*. Retrieved July 28, 2007, from www.americanchronicle.com.

Barker, J. *The Power of Vision*. Burnsville, Minnesota: Chart House Learning, 1993.

Belf, T. *Coaching with Spirit*. San Francisco: Jossey-Bass/Pfeiffer, 2002.

Bianco-Mathis, V., L. Nabors, and C. Roman. *Leading From the Inside Out: A Coaching Model*. Thousand Oaks, California: Sage Publications, 2002.

———. *The Dialogue Deck*. Vienna, Virginia: Strategic Performance Group, 2007.

———. *The Organizational Coaching Model*. Retrieved October 1, 2007, from www.strategicperformance.net.

Boyatzis, R., and D. Goleman. *Emotional Competence Inventory*. Boston: HayGroup, 2001.

Briggs, K., and I. Briggs-Myers. *Myers-Briggs Type Indicator*. Mountain View, California: CPP, 1998.

Buckingham, M. *Go Put Your Strengths to Work*. New York: Free Press, 2007.

Burns, D. *Feeling Good: The New Mood Therapy*. New York: William Morrow, 1980.

Cavanaugh, M., and A. Grant. "Executive Coaching in Organizations: The Personal Is the Professional." *The International Journal of Coaching in Organizations*, volume 2, number 2, 2004.

Ellis, A. "The Practice of Rational-Emotive Therapy." *Theoretical and Empirical Foundations of Rational-Emotive Therapy*, A. Ellis and J. Whitely, editors. Monterey, California: Brooks/Cole, 1979.

Executive Coaching Forum. *The Executive Coaching Handbook* (3rd edition). 2007. Retrieved October 1, 2007, from www.executivecoachingforum.com.

Gaynes, S. "When Sales and Coaching Combine: An IBM Success Story." *ASTD in Practice*. Alexandria, Virginia: ASTD, 2004.

Grant, A. "What Is Evidence-Based Executive Workplace and Life Coaching?" Keynote Address at First Evidence-Based Coaching Conference. Australia: University of Sydney, July 2003.

Hargrove, R. *Masterful Coaching.* Revised Edition. San Francisco: Jossey-Bass, 1995.

———. *Masterful Coaching.* San Francisco: Jossey-Bass, 2000.

International Coach Federation. *ICF Ethical Guidelines.* Lexington, Kentucky: International Coach Federation, 2006. Retrieved October 1, 2007, from www.coachfederation.org.

Leonard, T. *CleanSweep.* Coach U, 1998.

Lombardo, M., and R. Eichinger. *The Career Architect.* Minneapolis: Lominger, 1992.

McArthur, P., R. Putnam, and D. Smith. *Ladder of Inference.* 1999. Retrieved October 1, 2007, from www.actiondesign.com/resources/concepts/ladder_intro.htm.

O'Neill, M. *Executive Coaching With Backbone and Heart.* San Francisco: John Wiley & Sons, 2000.

Phillips, J., and P. Phillips. "Measuring ROI in Executive Coaching." *The International Journal of Coaching in Organizations*, volume 3, number 1, 2005.

Reynolds, M. "Alfred Adler and Coaching." *The International Journal of Coaching in Organizations*, issue 1, 2006.

Rock, D. *Quiet Leadership.* New York: HarperCollins Publishers, 2006.

———. *Workplace Coaching.* Sydney, Australia: Results Coaching Systems. Retrieved June 1, 2007, from www.workplacecoaching.com.

Schwartz, J., and B. Beyette. *Free Yourself from Obsessive-Compulsive Behavior.* New York: Regan Books, 1996.

Schwartz, J., and S. Begley. *The Mind and the Brain: Neuroplasticity and the Power of Mental Force.* New York: HarperCollins Publishers, 2002.

Senge, Peter et al. *The Fifth Discipline Fieldbook.* New York: Doubleday, 1994.

Staub, R. *The Heart of Leadership.* Provo, Utah: Executive Excellence, 2002.

Stober, D. "Approaches to Research on Executive and Organizational Coaching Outcomes." *The International Journal of Coaching in Organizations*, volume 3, number 1, 2005.

Stober, D., and A. Grant, editors. *Evidence-Based Coaching Handbook.* Hoboken, New Jersey: John Wiley & Sons, 2006.

Thomas, K., and R. Kilmann. *Thomas-Kilmann Conflict Mode Instrument.* Mountain View, California: Xicom, 1974.

Whitworth, L., K. Kimsey-House, H. Kimsey-House, and P. Sandahl. *Co-Active Coaching* (1st edition). Mountain View, California: Davies-Black Publishers, 1998.

———. *Co-Active Coaching* (2nd edition). Mountain View, California: Davies-Black Publishers, 2007.

Zeus, P., and S. Skiffington. *The Complete Guide to Coaching at Work.* Sydney, Australia: McGraw-Hill, 2000.

About the Authors

With over 20 years of experience and a doctorate in human resource and organization development, **Virginia Bianco-Mathis** is considered a leader in her field. Her background includes a core set of industry positions, extensive consulting with corporate and agency executives, and publications and presentations in the areas of performance management, organizational change, leadership development, executive team building, coaching, and strategic planning.

Bianco-Mathis has held positions in human resources and organization development at C&P Telephone, AT&T, Lockheed Martin, and the Artery Organization. Presently, she is a professor in the School of Business and the department chair of Management Programs at Marymount University. She teaches courses in organization development, team and group dynamics, leadership, and strategy. She is also a partner with the Strategic Performance Group. Her present consulting engagements include leadership development, executive coaching, strategic planning, team building, and organizational change.

Bianco-Mathis has given presentations at several international conferences, including such titles as A Multidisciplinary Approach to Implementing Total Quality and Change: Best Practices. Her journal publications include "Consulting Dilemmas" in *Training and Development Journal*, "Cross-Functional Teams at AOL" in *OD Practitioner*, "Learn to Speak IT: OD Consulting Within the World of Technology" in *ASTD Links—Consultants in Practice*, and numerous articles for the *Washington Business Journal*. Her book publications include *Faculty Handbook*, *Change in Organizations: Best Practices*, *Leading From the Inside Out: A Coaching Model*, and *The Dialogue Deck*.

Lisa Nabors is a partner with Strategic Performance Group and is recognized by the International Coach Federation as a professional certified coach. Nabors often presents on the topic of coaching to industry and professional groups. She began coaching while pursuing a 16-year stint as a senior-level human resource/training and development professional in private industry. Her passion is in optimizing individual, team, and organization performance, and her coaching clients include managers, executives, and teams in organizations such as America Online, AARP, American Registry for Internet Numbers, Kaiser Permanente, the U.S. Department of Education, and the U.S. Environmental Protection Agency. Nabors' expertise includes gathering and feeding back data, cutting to the core issues, helping clients consider choices, and creating action plans designed to achieve specific, measurable results.

Nabors is a certified user of all Center for Creative Leadership 360 degree feedback instruments, the BarOn EQi and EQ 360, LEI, APT 360 Instruments, Myers-Briggs Type Indicator, and many other customized instruments. Nabors earned her bachelor of arts and master of education degrees from the University of Maryland where she also completed doctoral level coursework on leadership effectiveness. In 2007, she served as subject matter expert and editor for the ASTD Coaching Certificate Program and delivered the program to an international class prior to ASTD's International Conference and Exposition in Atlanta, Georgia. She is an adjunct faculty member for Marymount University and George Washington University, and she is the co-author of *The Dialogue Deck* and *Leading From the Inside Out: A Coaching Model.*

Cynthia H. Roman is an executive coach and organization development professional who coaches, trains, and consults in a variety of organizations, including federal, not-for-profit, higher education, and professional services sectors. She has assisted organizations with critical management and leadership issues, such as coaching, mentoring, executive presence, leadership development, communication, conflict management, team development, supervision, and performance management.

Roman founded the Graduate Certificate Program in Leadership Coaching at the George Washington University (GWU), and she often gives presentations on coaching topics. She also teaches in GWU's Center for Excellence in Public Leadership. Roman is co-author of *Leading From the Inside Out: A Coaching Model.*

Roman earned her bachelor of arts degree with distinction from the University of Virginia, master's degree in counseling from the University of Georgia, and doctoral degree in adult education from Virginia Polytechnic Institute and State University. Roman has served as an adjunct faculty member of GWU, University of North Carolina at Pembroke, University of Maryland University College, Marymount University, and National-Louis University.

Index